No Brighter Dawn

No Brighter Dawn

Vincent G. De Young

America's Sunrise
April 19, 1775

The Battle of Lexington and Paul Revere's Ride

Minutemen Virtues and Values for all Time

Illustrated

Patriot 1775 Publishing
Grand Rapids, Michigan

ebook ISBN 978-1-105-86499-5

Print Book ISBN 978-1-4717-4230-9

Hardback ISBN 978-0-578-10414-0

Vincent G. De Young
Grand Rapids, Michigan

HIGHLIGHTS FROM

NO BRIGHTER DAWN

"So on April 19, 1775, the morning skies in the colonial province of Massachusetts Bay brightened, from long, pre-dawn, horizontal streaks of red and gray, to bright orange, to clear blue, then into a beautifully clear and cool spring day—and the American Revolutionary War began."

"About midnight, pulling back tightly on the reins of heavily-breathing Brown Beauty whose hooves were pounding deep into the wet, dirt road, Paul Revere came to a jarring halt directly in front of Rev. Clarke's parsonage in Lexington."

"After several minutes, as the men and teenage boys were running back to the Common, individually and in small groups, a mass of British Regulars suddenly appeared in the distance, about a quarter mile toward the east, on the road that turned toward the Common. The sun behind them was straining to rise; sunrise was 4:57 a.m."

"The Lexington minutemen were not aggressors; rather they wanted and sought a secure peace--the peace of enjoying freedom--that was earned by standing against, at the cost of sacrificing their own lives, those who wanted the "peace" of brute force."

"With the minutemen, reliability is shown in their almost universal willingness to "be there" and "do it" regardless of the hour or sacrifice that was necessary and despite the dangers that were waiting."

"If you set aside this book for a moment and gaze out a window toward whatever nature you can see (a tree, a field, a garden, a flower, a child at play) and then close your eyes and imagine a New England meetinghouse full of worshippers, you may be able to hear, deep in your heart, the Lexington congregation, gathered together, powerfully and distinctly singing "*O God Our Help in Ages Past*" on Sunday morning, April 14, 1775."

With love to my children and grandchildren

Contents

Acknowledgements xix

Prologue xxi

Historical Landscape of the 1700s................................. xxvii

Part I. The Day... 1

    Chapter 1. An April Sunrise.................................... 3

                   The Year... 3

                   The Time and Place in History 4

                   Historic Importance for America 5

                   Universal Meaning of that Sunrise........ 6

    Chapter 2. Midnight Warning 9

                   Destination Lexington 9

                   The New British Laws........................ 14

                   War on the Horizon 16

                   Paul Revere in Boston....................... 17

                   The Old North Church 19

                   Assignment: Lexington 22

                   Two Lanterns.................................... 23

                   The Road to Lexington 26

                   Capture of Paul Revere 30

    Chapter 3. The Common.................................... 33

                   A Green Triangle 33

The Lexington Militia................................34

Captain Parker..35

Chapter 4. America's Sunrise..............................37

Call to the Common................................37

Dismissal at 3:00 a.m. 39

"They Are Here!"....................................40

Facing the Regulars 40

No Brighter Dawn 41

Submission to the King.........................43

The First Shot..45

Jonas Parker Fights Back....................49

Those Who Fell For Their Country 49

Concord..50

Battle Road...54

Part II. Minutemen Virtues and Values.............................57

Chapter 5. Admirable Courage..............................59

The First Virtue......................................59

A Different Kind of Courage.................60

Captain Parker's Courage 61

Jonas Parker's Courage 65

Jedediah Munroe—a Very Special
Courage...66

Courage of the Old 67

Courage on April 19, 1775—
Lessons for Today..............................68
   Defense of Justified Values...........68
   The Standard of Admirable
   Courage 69

Self-Defense and Scripture 70

The "Governing Authorities"
in 1775 71

Admirable Courage and
Interpersonal Actions 72

Intentional Violence in Athletics
and Entertainment 73

Chapter 6. Purposeful Moral Unity 75

Unity in 1775 75

Women and Men Unified for Liberty ... 76

African American Unity with the
Patriots 77

Prince Estabrook 77

A Brave African American Woman 78

Unity of the Minutemen 79

Purposeful Moral Unity on April 19,
1775—Lessons for Today 79
Unity to Achieve a Common and
Worthy Goal 79

Today's Need for Purposeful
Moral Unity 81

Chapter 7. Virtuous Reliability 83

Examples of Reliability in 1775 83
Sam Adams—Leader of the
Revolution, Patriarch of Liberty,
and a Founding Father 84

A Futile Attempt at Bribery 86

Sam Adams in History 87

John Hancock 90

Paul Revere 95

The Minutemen 96

Virtuous Reliability on April 19, 1775—Lessons for Today 96

Chapter 8. The Desire for Secure Peace 99

A Unique and Inspirational Perspective on Peace......................... 99

Winning a Secure Peace 100

Lessons for Today 101
　Secure Peace Must be Earned. ... 101
　Secure Peace Through Meetings.................................... 101
　Working and Standing for Secure Peace.............................. 102
　Secure Peace Through Unity 103
　Gaining Allies for Secure Peace.. 103
　Patience and Gaining Secure Peace. 104
　Kindness and Gaining Secure Peace. 104

Chapter 9. Noble Freedom 107

Freedom From Arbitrary Power 107

What Noble Freedom Means and Does Not Mean Based on Minutemen Values 109

Chapter 10. Radiating Faith 111

Religion in 1700 New England.......... 111

The Puritan Heritage—The Covenant 114

Belief in God............................... 116

Faith in Scripture 118

Belief in Prayer 120
　Prayer Before Battle.................... 121

Going to the Meetinghouse 122
    Hymns of the Minutemen 122

    O God Our Help in Ages Past 125

Going to Church (the
Meetinghouse) and the Revolution ... 126

Radiating Faith on April 19, 1775—
Lessons for Today 127
    The Wellspring of Minutemen
    Virtues and Values 128

    Why Not Today? 128

    Strengths of Pluralities 129

    A New Sunrise for America 130

Bibliography and Sources 133

Illustrations

Statue of Lexington Minuteman xx

Hendrik de Jonge, 1922 xxii

Portrait of Ben Franklin xxviii

Portrait of Isaac Newton xxix

Portrait of Voltaire xxxi

Statue of Mozart xxxiv

Portrait of Beethoven xxxiv

Early Colonial Home (similar to residence of Rev. Jonas Clarke) 11

Sketch of Boston in 1775 13

Paul Revere on horseback 18

Old North Church 21

Old North Church as seen in Boston's North End today 25

Statue of Paul Revere by Old North Church 29

The Buckman Tavern as restored today 38

Sunrise as it may have looked on April 19, 1775 42

Sketch by author of Lexington Common at sunrise, April 19, 1775 44

Engraving of the Battle of Lexington 45

British Regulars Attacking (reenactment) 48

Concord's Old North Bridge (reconstructed) 52

The "grassy hillside" looking down on Concord's Old North Bridge 53

Statue of George Washington on horseback 56

New England Farm 62

Portrait of Sam Adams..85

Thomas Jefferson (Mt. Rushmore) 89

John Hancock's Signature on Declaration of Independence 91

John Hancock Tower in Boston 93

John Hancock Building in Chicago 94

New England Church..113

Bible, open to the Book of Genesis..................................119

Statue of Isaac Watts...124

Acknowledgements

Many books have been written about the American Revolutionary War and about the people who lived that history. A number of the historical accounts are noted in the bibliography at the end of this book. The accounts in the bibliography are informative and well-written—and capture the history in excellent detail, describing both positive and negative aspects of the personalities and events of that time. I owe a great deal to these sources for factual information used in this book. In particular, Arthur B. Tourtellot's book on Lexington and Concord and David Hackett Fischer's book on Paul Revere meticulously describe the details of the beginning of the Revolutionary War.

For historical information, I also relied on original sources, including the depositions of most of the minutemen who fought at Lexington, Paul Revere's deposition given in 1775 and his letter written in 1798, and the eyewitness account of Rev. Jonas Clarke, the Lexington minister, written in 1776. Most of the quotations in this book are excerpts from speeches and writings of patriots and leaders of that time, including George Washington, Thomas Jefferson, Sam Adams, John Adams, Patrick Henry, and Thomas Paine.

For assistance in completing this book, I am indebted to Ryan Voogt (my son-in-law), currently working on his Doctorate in History, for reading the manuscript and providing helpful information, insight, and correction of various errors (in writing and in substance). He encouraged me to highlight the great importance of the key motivating principle of the minutemen. I would also like to thank my daughter, Donna De Young, for reading the manuscript and giving practical advice concerning the content. Any errors in the book are solely my responsibility.

Statue of Lexington Minuteman

Prologue

The American Revolutionary War was difficult, bloody, very long, and very tragic in many ways. It has not been my intent to glorify the War. However, the War was, in my judgment and in the opinion of many others, necessary—and it accomplished just and enduring results. Today, millions upon millions enjoy the lasting positive benefits and blessings of that struggle without even realizing it—and many are not the least appreciative or even cognizant of the people and the moral principles that made the Revolution successful and the freedom we now have possible.

An important purpose of the book, then, is to recount, using my own thoughts and in my own words with a moderate degree of literary freedom, the first day of the American Revolutionary War in a new, inspiring, and positive light. Beyond a description of the first day of that war, an underlying premise for this book is that the most important value of history is what lessons we can learn from it—and then applying those lessons constructively to our own lives and our own time.

Consistent with this premise, this book, unlike many other historical narratives, attempts not only to tell a true story but to apply that story, the story of minutemen virtues and values, to our generation and to the future. For this reason, the book is divided into two parts. Part I is an account of the first day of the War and surrounding historical events. Part II describes the positive lessons of that history that can be applied to our day and to future generations. I have done my best to ensure the historical information in both Parts I and II is consistent with published history and original sources.

My desire to be positive about the American Revolution comes from my background and, probably most important, from my own heritage. Though not born in the United States, my parents were true American patriots with the full force of the meaning of those words. As many other immigrants from Europe, my father, born and raised on a farm in Holland, crossed the Atlantic "to come to America." In 1922, Hendrik de Jonge, age nineteen, alone, knowing

Hendrik de Jonge in 1922

no English, and gripping a few Dutch "guilder" in his pocket, disembarked from an ocean steamer at Hoboken, New Jersey. The youngest of fifteen children, he was the only one to immigrate to the United States. An ambitious, physically strong, and determined man, with basic principles, instilled by godly parents, already set in concrete, he came for freedom to "get ahead" and a "new start" from whatever experiences had set him back in Holland. In those years, it apparently was very difficult in European countries, having unwritten class cultures, to break through social barriers to achieve one's dream. And my father had dreams—or I should say goals—to accomplish. In simple terms, as he told me himself, he wanted to "make something of himself"—his own version of the pursuit of happiness. He did just that.

My mother, Jemima de Waal Malefyt, whom my father met soon after arriving in America, also came from Holland—but as an infant in 1902. Her parents, like my father, came for a new start and to do what they wanted to do, which in their case was to own their own greenhouse and nursery business. My mother's father, born in 1861, had a natural and self-taught expertise in flowers, plants, and trees. Having been driven out of South Africa by victorious British forces during the Boer War (1899–1902), my grandparents could not find in Holland, their birthplace, the opportunity and happiness they sought. They found it in the United States of America, in New Jersey, achieving their goal of establishing a nursery business and also raising thirteen children.

My mother and father loved and appreciated the United States. It gave them all they had in this world. They appreciated the freedom—freedom to work, own your own business, and "get ahead" with your own effort and education—and especially the privilege of voting (they considered voting a solemn duty and high honor that they would never, not for anything, skip doing). In addition, they felt it their duty (and enjoyment) to participate in, contribute to, and lead many groups and associations in society.

Learning English rapidly, my father soon noticed and took advantage of the opportunities in America for self-help education. While working ten hours a day as a laborer, he went to night school and took correspondence courses, learning the basics of home construction, drafting blueprints, residential heating systems, and electrical wiring. Awake at 3:00 a.m. to pore over his books and assignments without distraction, he soon gained a reputation as a "hardworking Dutchman." My mother was a good match for my father. Gentle and kind, tolerant, well-read, a musician and poet, and skilled in raising children, homemaking, letter writing, quilting, and prayer, she was the file for softening my father's sharp edges.

Soon after their marriage in 1925, my parents settled in Prospect Park, New Jersey, a small, mainly Dutch, enclave. Using his new-found knowledge acquired in night school and correspondence courses, in the early 1930s my father started, with the indispensable help of my mother as bookkeeper, a small home heating and contracting business (Modern Installation Company—it later also delivered home fuel oil) that over the years provided steady employment to many people. It was called "Modern" because the business specialized in converting home heating systems from coal-fired furnaces to oil burners, which was a new technological cycle in the 1930s and 1940s. Through years of stick-to-it effort, setbacks, and struggle including the Depression, the business grew and prospered—allowing them to support their large family and, of prime importance, provide them with a Christian education.

My parents were Christians—Dutch Christian Reformed Calvinists—believing in the Bible, faithful church attendance (twice on Sunday), and Christian education from kindergarten through college. Though far from perfect, they did their best to follow God's will including, in particular, all the Ten Commandments. When researching this book, I discovered they had much in common with the New England Puritans of the 1700s. Growing up, it was not difficult to sense my parents' deep obligation to try to do what is right as they understood the laws of America and the principles of the Bible.

When the United States entered World War II, my father, then 38, had a wife and seven children at home and was not a candidate for active military service. Nonetheless, wanting to do something for the country he appreciated so much, he enlisted in the New Jersey National Guard and spent many weekends training for possible active service "in case he was needed."

I and my three brothers and three sisters were raised in this heritage, though not always living up to it. Yet, we appreciated and used the opportunities provided in the United States, including the Christian education our parents were so strongly committed to. My sisters June, Arlene, and Lucretia, highly accomplished and "participators" in their own right, married military veterans. My brothers and I each enlisted in the military services. My two older brothers, Hank and Karl, served in the United States Air Force while my twin brother, Vic, served in the United States Army. With college completed and emulating my two older brothers, I joined the Air Force for a five-year tour of duty. Looking back, I now know my mother's faithful prayers got me through those youthful and risky years. In missions to destinations in much of the world, I never found any place even close to the blessings of the U.S.A.

After the Air Force, assisted by my wife, Carol, and encouraged by my parents who had ingrained in me that higher education was the key to "getting ahead nowadays," I was given the opportunity to complete the education I needed for a career in law. Soon thereafter Carol earned her RN, BSN, and MSN degrees preparing her for a career in nursing. The education and training we received allowed us to raise six very special children and have wonderful grandchildren as rich blessings besides.

So, by God's grace, at heart and in my life I am a Christian and also an American Patriot. Although life, as for all of us, has offered difficult experiences, I am convinced and grateful that I, like millions of others, have been afforded opportunities and the blessings of God in America that, as my father used to say, are "much more than we deserve." I also believe in the "Covenant of Grace" (considered in chapter ten of this book). Without God's grace, there would be no blessings of liberty and no United States of America.

Historical Landscape of the 1700s

To understand the context of the American Revolutionary War that started in 1775, 237 years ago, it is helpful to review the historical landscape of Europe and America during that period of Western world history. The 1700s were years of important changes and events—in science, political affairs, religion, and culture. The consequences of these changes and events proved to be far reaching, affecting world history and everyday life for centuries to come.

In science, two of several key advancements were in electricity and steam power. Electricity, its powers scientifically observed in the 1600s, was first controlled in experiments in the 1700s. The use of steam for power, first discovered in the late 1600s, became a practical reality in the 1700s when the first usable steam engine was invented. These discoveries contributed to the Industrial Revolution of the 1800s and formed two of the building blocks of current-day life and society—the pervasive use of electricity throughout civilization and the transformation of human transportation, from the horse on land and the wind on the sea, to manmade machines.

Benjamin Franklin, 1706-1790. American Founding Father and Inventor. His experiments in electricity gave him the knowledge to invent the lightning rod.

A third major advance in science was the invention, in the late 1700s in America, of the cotton gin. Strangely enough, this positive development had a serious negative "unintended consequence"—it dramatically increased the production of cotton, which, while strengthening the economy of the South in the United States, also intensified the importance and use (and abuse) of slaves for picking the cotton. This in turn increased the strength of the moral opposition to slavery, resulting in widespread calls for its abolition. So it could be said that the cotton gin was an indirect causative factor in the growth of, and ensuing opposition to, slavery, the principal cause of the American Civil War.

In Europe, the late 1600s and early 1700s saw the ascendancy of Isaac Newton's genius in mathematics and physics with his works on the law of gravity. Because his scientific formulas led to new conclusions about the universe, they had an indirect and unintentional, some might say negative, impact on religion and morality.

Sir Isaac Newton, 1642-1727. His formulas defined the law of gravity and contributed to the Age of Reason in the 1700s.

In governmental affairs, the 1700s in Europe began with few changes in the pre-existing, basically feudal, political system in which, although with increasing challenges, royalty and the aristocratic few governed the many. To be sure, a parliamentary system was functioning in England, but power was still shared with the monarchy—and parliament itself represented only about ten percent of the citizens. In other European countries, notably France and Spain, monarchies were essentially in control. The 1700s ended with revolutions, first in North America and then in France—giving birth to representative self-government followed by its slow and sometimes interrupted (in France with Napoleon and in America with the American Civil War) progress in the 1800s. These revolutions and ensuing democracies became the source or guide (or inspiration) for modern-day democratic government in much of the Western world.

Concerning religion and culture, people in Europe and America in the 1700s experienced the zenith of the Age of Reason or "The Enlightenment." The Age of Reason, championed by the deistic French philosopher Voltaire and relying on scientific discoveries including the evidence of Newton's formulas related to gravity, essentially taught that mankind by reason and science could determine ultimate truth. Armed with this truth, it was believed human beings could thereby vastly improve their life and social relations and even achieve perfect happiness with minimal or even no resort to faith in God. It was the beginning of Secularism. As to faith in God, it was summarily dismissed by many philosophers of The Enlightenment—the thinking then seemed to be that perhaps a god created the universe but had no daily involvement in men's affairs.

Voltaire, 1694-1778, French philosopher who taught the supremacy of science and man's reasoning over religion.

Voltaire's influence was strong in Europe, but in America, in the 1700s, it seemed more indirect and quite diluted—for example both Ben Franklin and Thomas Jefferson had deistic and Enlightenment leanings, but there is ample proof they believed that the God of the Bible directed the affairs of men and the destinies of nations. It should be noted that, in time, the Age of Reason did eventually influence many in America—but this was many years after the American Revolution.

A positive result of the Age of Reason for the American Revolution was the teachings of the English philosopher and rationalist John Locke, who wrote extensively about government in the late 1600s. He concluded that government's main purpose was the protection of individual freedom. Although Locke was not well known by the common people in America, his views had a strong influence on leading American patriots.

The Age of Reason also produced another positive force for the American Revolution. This was Thomas Paine, a brilliant Englishman turned ardent American patriot who marched with Washington's Army after he immigrated to America. In his widely read pamphlet, *Common Sense*, he wrote that America's revolutionary break with England was perfectly justified for an array of irrefutable reasons. His strong logical reasoning seemed finally to convince and inspire almost everyone in America as to the justice of the War—except for those Loyalists (loyal to the British Crown) who were beyond the point of no return and one religious group (which will remain unnamed but it was not the Puritans or any other major Protestant denomination). This objecting religious group, unlike other Protestants, clung with a bull-dog grip to their apparent belief that no rebellion against any king was ever justified for any reason. In his fashion, Paine took the occasion to use highly logical reasoning, including scripture, to refute their position.

The Great Awakening religious revival of the 1700s (called the "Awakening" in Europe), which might be considered a second "Reformation" (not a reform of the organized church but a reaction to the secular conclusions of the Age of Reason), had its roots in the extensive Piety Movement in Europe in the 1600s. The Piety Movement had a significant influence on Protestants. The Pietists emphasized the need for spiritual conversion and living a devout, biblically based, Christian life to prove it. With Christian teachers and preachers like the Englishmen John Wesley and George Whitefield and the great American theologian Jonathan Edwards, The Great Awakening in America in the mid-1700s did the same—but often with greater stress on salvation or spiritual rebirth. The Great Awakening's teaching of conversion and Christian virtues revitalized and validated New England Puritanism, with one major difference: The beliefs of the Puritans, relying on a mutual "covenant" with God and with each other, decidedly reached into their political life, where both political and religious freedom were considered essential.

In the fields of art and music, the 1700s were by no means primitive or backward. In art, the mid-1700s saw the development of "Neoclassicism"—basically a revival of classical Greek and Roman art but with an emphasis on high clarity, detail in expression, and "educated idealism." America's main contributor to this period of art history was John Trumbull. A portrait artist of immense talent, his paintings give us exacting detail of events and personalities of the American Revolution, including "The Surrender of Cornwallis" and Trumbull's masterpiece depicting in precise strokes the signing of the Declaration of Independence. John Trumbull himself served in the American Revolutionary War.

In music, perhaps the greatest composers that ever lived and classical music of unsurpassed beauty stem from the 1700s. In 1775, Mozart was 19 and by that time had already composed over forty symphonies. Beethoven, born in 1770, published his first composition in 1782. Handel wrote "The Messiah" in 1741 (in 24 days!). Franz Joseph Haydn, perhaps the father of classical music, was born in 1732 and composed over 100 symphonies.

Wolfgang Amadeus Mozart, 1756–1791. In 1775 he was 19 and by then already a famous composer, pianist, and violinist.

Ludwig van Beethoven.

Ludwig van Beethoven, 1770–1827. Perhaps the greatest composer of all time, he was born before the American Revolutionary War started.

Returning to the field of government and politics, the 1700s saw the consolidation of British power in North America. In contrast, the previous two centuries were times of European exploration (the 1500s) and colonization (the 1600s). These 200 years of exploration and then colonization and settlement in North America involved the strenuous and often violent efforts of several competing nations, the main players being England, Spain, and France. In the 1700s, the bitter competition among these powers both in America and in Europe culminated in the Seven Years War, which was actually fought among several European powers. In America it was called the French and Indian War, pitting England (and its colonies) against the French and their Indian allies. The war ended in 1763.

In a nutshell, so far as America was concerned, England won the French and Indian War—resulting in British dominance of Canada and most of North America east of the Mississippi River. The thirteen American colonies, already long established under the British Crown and protected by the British in the War, had survived intact and were included in this part of the British Empire.

Since the 1600s, the English colonies in America had been given significant political freedom, via royal and commercial charters, to elect their own legislatures or assemblies and to control the judiciary by determining and paying their salaries. And more than 50 percent of the people in the colonies in the mid to late 1700s were not of English descent. As a result, America already had become a "great melting pot"—producing solid ingots who, for the most part even by world standards of the present day, were highly civilized, literate, self-reliant, and resourceful people.

However, the colonies were still subject to the laws of the English Parliament and approved by the King. These included regulation and taxation of trade and commerce including duties on imports and exports. The British King retained the right to veto laws enacted by colonial legislatures and also appointed most of the colonial governors who in turn had considerable power over internal matters in America. Trade with other countries was largely prohibited by the British, but colonists often sidestepped these trade restrictions by extensive smuggling.

So in 1763, England found itself with immense power, responsibilities, and opportunities in North America. It also had sustained huge debts to win the Seven Years War. To consolidate British power and administer its far-flung responsibilities, the English Parliament decided that the American colonies would have to provide more money to support its military security and to help pay for the costs of the war (which, after all, it was asserted, had preserved the colonies). An unspoken purpose behind British trade and tax laws was to provide the mother country with more commercial benefits, i.e., profits for English companies and for the British treasury.

The idea of using colonies for the benefit of gaining wealth, securing, and enlarging a European nation's empire, sometimes called mercantilism, was not new. But the methods chosen by the British in the 1760s were painfully direct and more obvious than before—and were meant to be strictly enforced. One of the methods selected was to increase tax revenues, from a variety of sources, flowing from the American colonies but without thought of obtaining their consent. The King and his successive prime ministers were in agreement with this course of action. They saw taxation of the colonies as completely consistent with past policy and quite fair for all concerned.

This in very general and brief terms is a sketch of the historical landscape relevant to America and England at the time of the American "Revolution"—that is to say, the widespread, strong, and continuing opposition to the new British laws—which started in earnest in 1765. Organized, active, military resistance and fighting, the American Revolutionary War itself, started ten years later. The ultimate outcome of the War, accomplished even before it was officially over, was the Declaration of Independence and the beginning of the United States of America.

Having considered this overview of the 1700s, we now turn our eyes to the first day of that War.

Part I

The Day

Chapter One

An April Sunrise

May this day be remembered to the glory of God and our own instruction and improvement, so long as we live.

—Rev. Jonas Clarke, Lexington Minister in 1775

The sun never shined on a cause of greater worth.

—Thomas Paine

Sunrise, April 19! How many Americans understand and appreciate its significance? If July 4 represents the enduring expression of American freedom, then sunrise on April 19 stands for the courageous beginning of the long and costly seven-year struggle for that freedom. It could well be that, without the incomparable courage of a band of valiant "embattled farmers" at that April dawn, American independence would never have happened. The American Revolutionary War, which led to freedom and government "by the people," started its momentous and arduous journey precisely at the rising of the sun on that day. That dawn was "America's Sunrise," and its fight for freedom can be measured from that hour.

No seers were they, but simple men;
Its vast results the future hid
The meaning of the work they did
Was strange and dark and doubtful then.

—John Greenleaf Whittier

In addition to its historic and essential importance for the existence of the United States, the American Revolutionary War, although its "vast results" were not recognized at the time, was the beginning of a universal struggle for the principles of human liberty, self-government, and freedom from autocratic rule that continues to this day. It was not simply a North American uprising. In the words of Thomas Jefferson, "it was monarchy and not merely British monarchy" that was opposed.

And as penned by the poet John Greenleaf Whittier one hundred years later, the sacrifice of those who fell at that Lexington sunrise "shook the feudal tower"—forever ending automatic submissiveness to despotism, while enlightening the world to the ideal of self-determination. In the full spectrum of civilization, that April sunrise, that day and the virtues and values that inspired that time in America, are of enduring importance and meaning—for all people, for all ages to come.

The Time and Place in History

The year was 1775. The place was Lexington—a small village of 750 American colonists, or "provincials" as they were then called, in the eastern part of the Royal Province of Massachusetts-Bay in Colonial British America, twelve miles west of Boston. Most residents of Lexington lived in a scattering of small homes and farmhouses spreading out for several miles from the town's center. On the previous evening of Tuesday, April 18, the weather in eastern Massachusetts was gradually, almost imperceptibly, cooling after an unseasonably warm but rainy day. As the April night's full darkness waited for dawn, a strong breeze of fresh cooler air began flowing from the west—perhaps an omen of the impending revolutionary struggle.

So on April 19, 1775, the morning skies in the colonial province of Massachusetts-Bay brightened, from long, pre-dawn, horizontal streaks of red and gray, to bright orange, to clear blue, then into a beautifully clear and cool spring day— and the American Revolutionary War began. Yes, there were many confrontations, alarms, and even violent outbursts before this sunrise. But the morning battle at Lexington was the first engagement in the Revolution involving armed conflict between attacking British Regulars and organized American militia. In John Adams' mind, the Revolution turned "from the pen to the sword" at the battle of Lexington.

What a glorious day for America!

—Sam Adams, April 19, 1775

Historic Importance for America

The battle of Lexington undoubtedly ranks among the most important events of American history. Although armed conflict was anticipated as inevitable by some American patriot leaders, the attack by the British and the armed resistance by the militia, both at Lexington and later that day at Concord, shocked and "woke up" the American people in the same way that future startling events would—the shelling of Fort Sumter in 1861 that began the Civil War, the sinking of the battleship Maine in 1898 that started the Spanish-American War, the bombing of Pearl Harbor in 1941 that began American involvement in World War II, and the terror attacks of 9/11 that led to America's total effort in the War Against Terror.

The scale of the battle of Lexington itself seems very small compared to many of these later events. But in 1775, when news of the battle had quickly spread through the colonies, Americans were stunned —and were brought, suddenly and forcibly, to the realization that the war had started for real, and that it would be an armed and difficult struggle for liberty by the seemingly weak and unorganized colonists against a powerful empire. And all Americans would be involved in some way.

No man was a warmer wisher for reconciliation than myself before the fatal nineteenth of April 1775, but the moment the event of that day was made known, I rejected the hardened, sullen tempered Pharaoh of England forever.

—Thomas Paine

Moreover, as all attacks on America have done, the assault by the British Regulars at Lexington gripped the deep emotions of the nation—stirring up widespread patriotic fervor and rousing national anger and a desire for revenge. The "die was cast," as John Adams wrote. Americans who longed for freedom were united and world history made its momentous turn toward self-determination.

Universal Meaning of that Sunrise

Sunrise on April 19, 1775, stands for dependable men and women, in unity, holding firmly to their belief in democracy and liberty; for minutemen and militia, teenagers to men in their sixties, leaving their houses and beds in pre-dawn hours and running to the crucible of danger to defend their homes and families; and for the courage of seventy-seven vastly outnumbered citizen-soldiers, at five o'clock in the chill of morning, facing the unknown, and maybe death, on the Common in Lexington—and who were willing, but only if attacked, to fight advancing redcoated regiments of British Regulars, the King's Troops.

All that was theirs to give, they gave,
The flowers that blossomed from their grave
Have sown themselves beneath all skies.

—John Greenleaf Whittier

Yet there is another legacy of that sunrise. That morning and that day also reflect worthy and enduring universal virtues and values that are "beneath all skies." These are not solely American in nature or origin, but they were lived and carried out through shining examples by those Americans who participated in the struggle in those early morning hours and during that day and time.

Whether America shall long preserve her freedom or not
will depend on her virtue.

—Sam Adams

This book, centering on the battle of Lexington and surrounding history, is a brief story of these events written in the author's own words and reflecting his viewpoint. It honors the actions of the men and women who lived that early American history, including not only those who were in Lexington but also those who fought at Concord and during the British retreat to Boston that spring day.

Of equal or even greater importance, this book honors the foundational virtues and values, firmly held in the hearts of early American patriots, that inspired those who fought at Lexington and Concord and other patriots. Their efforts, even at the cost of their own lives, enabled the beginning of the United States of America. As explained in forthcoming chapters, these virtues and values being especially important in American history and in the continuing human struggle for freedom, are therefore given special identification for the purpose of this book. These are called:

Admirable Courage
Purposeful Moral Unity
Virtuous Reliability
The Desire for Secure Peace
Noble Freedom
Radiating Faith

If we fail to appreciate, apply, and preserve these virtues and values, the freedom we enjoy in America, in its noblest and most worthy sense, could well be endangered for our posterity and perhaps for the whole world.

We now turn to a narrative of the events in Eastern Massachusetts surrounding and including April 19, 1775. After considering these events, in Part II we will examine in closer detail the special virtues and values of that day. In other words, we will be uncovering and exploring the very building stones of America, "the land of the free." Hopefully we will be inspired to renew and rededicate ourselves to the great moral principles of that time.

Chapter Two
Midnight Warning

The fate of a nation was riding that night.

—Henry Wadsworth Longfellow, "Paul Revere's Ride"

Destination Lexington

In the first minutes of April 19, 1775, in the moonlit shadows of midnight, a single-minded and alert Paul Revere, on a muscular, heavily perspiring horse, came cantering at a "pretty smart pace" onto the unpaved roads of Lexington, Massachusetts, twelve miles west of Boston. His specific destination in Lexington, familiar to him because of earlier trips, was the home of Rev. Jonas Clarke, the minister for the Lexington Congregational Church and a strong and highly respected patriot. The Clarke residence, a large two-story wood-framed house of early colonial design, was less than a quarter mile west of the Lexington "Common."

Staying as guests with Rev. Clarke and his family (he had ten children at home) were both Sam Adams and John Hancock—the acknowledged leaders of the patriots in Boston and of all New England. Both men were well-known throughout the colonies and in England. They were then under threat of arrest by British governing authorities in Boston. Because of this, Adams and Hancock had fled Boston and were staying temporarily in Lexington, out of sight of British military forces, before traveling to Philadelphia to attend a meeting of the then-illegal second

Continental Congress representing the American colonies. So by chance, two of the most influential leaders of colonial resistance in Boston and New England and perhaps in all of America—both of whom, in a short fourteen months, were to be signers of the Declaration of Independence and, after the War, the first and second governors of the new State of Massachusetts—were, in the early morning hours of April 19, in the town of Lexington about 1,200 feet from where the American Revolutionary War started!

Early colonial home resembling the residence of Rev. Jonas Clarke in Lexington. Sam Adams and John Hancock were staying at Rev. Clarke's house on the night of April 18-19, 1775, when Paul Revere delivered his message that the Regulars were out.

Having looked at this snapshot of the first moments of April 19, 1775, we now step back and consider in greater detail the important events and places immediately leading up to and involving the historic sunrise on that day.

The chain of events began in Boston. Boston was then (and still is, of course) an important harbor city on the eastern coast of Massachusetts. However, because of subsequent man-made changes in the surrounding land and waterways, the present-day geography of the city of Boston is very different than in 1775. Then, except for a very narrow southerly strip of land—the "Boston Neck" connecting the city to the mainland—the city was contained within a small two-square-mile turtle-shaped island, its head pointed northeast. On the north side of the city opposite from the southern Neck side flowed the Charles River (more like a bay than a river). Directly north across that river from the Boston shore, less than a quarter mile, was Charlestown, also a city on a peninsula.

To the west of Charlestown about two miles, across the "Charlestown Neck" leading to the Massachusetts mainland, was the town of Cambridge. The Charles River to the immediate southwest of Charlestown and west of Boston was called the Back Bay. The coast of the Back Bay on the Cambridge side (opposite Boston's west shore) was marshland. This soft and wet coastline had an historical importance all its own—it would delay, with serious unintended consequences, the British military incursion into the countryside of Massachusetts on the night of April 18 and morning of April 19, 1775.

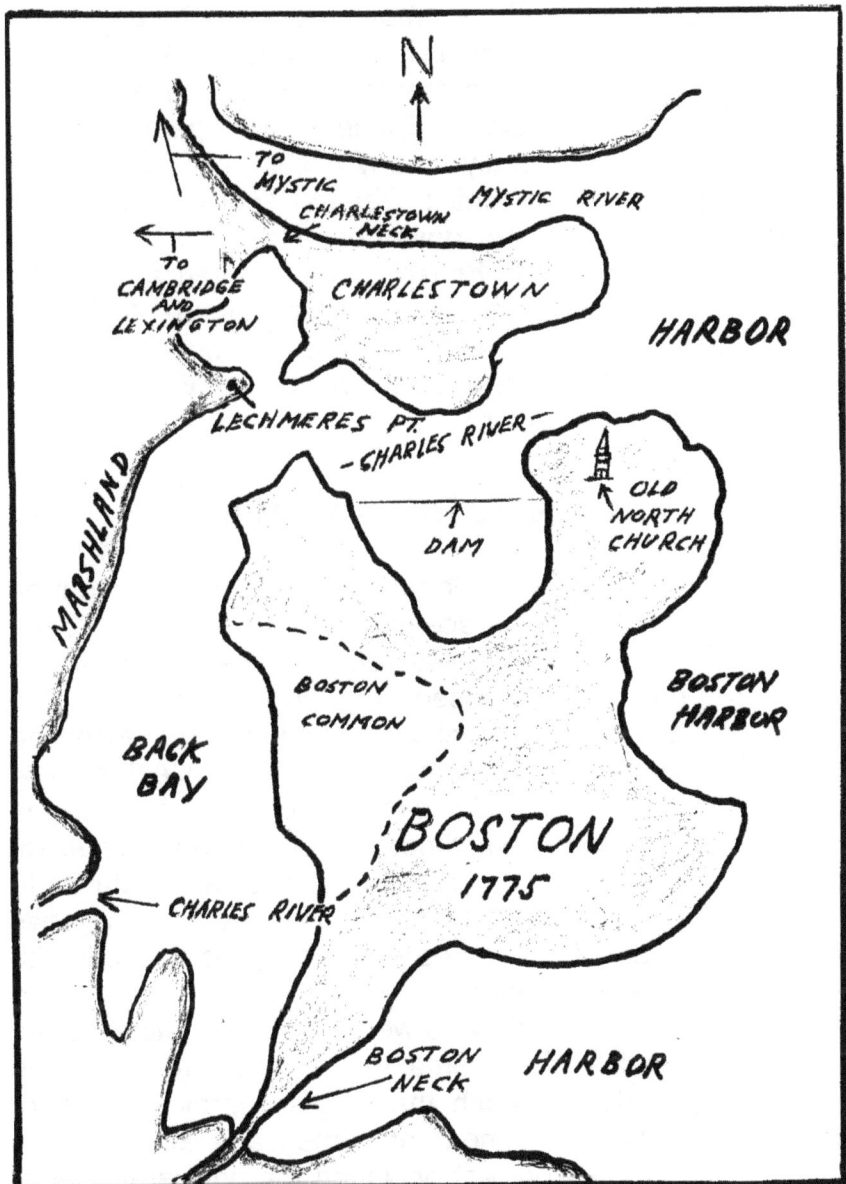

Boston on April 19, 1775. Sketch by author.

At this point in time, Boston was a closed port—forcibly closed by an act of the British Parliament as punishment for the Boston Tea Party sixteen months earlier (December 16, 1773). The city was under military occupation, enforced by 3,500 disciplined, but sometimes unruly and usually unhappy, British "Regulars." These troops, garrisoned far from home in an unfriendly, nearly hostile, city, were under the overall command of British General Thomas Gage, also serving as king-appointed governor of Massachusetts and commanding officer of all British forces in America. (General Gage also happened to be a military friend of George Washington—both had served together under General Edward Braddock in the French and Indian War that had ended twelve years earlier.)

The New British Laws

Backed by orders from London, General Gage was intent on firmly quelling the still-peaceable but nevertheless "open rebellion" in Massachusetts—a rebellion that, as in all the American colonies, opposed the increasingly punitive unilateral Acts of Parliament and royal decrees enforcing them. These measures, starting with the Sugar Act in 1764 and the Stamp Act in 1765, came across the Atlantic one after another, and sometimes were quickly repealed, modified, or not enforced in reaction to colonial resistance to the harshness and unpopularity of the laws. Those laws imposing new or different taxes were boycotted or evaded by almost everyone in America.

The torrent of British laws were all passed without input from the colonists and contained arbitrary requirements adopted by Parliament with the King's approval. Many of them were directly aimed at American liberty—these included the Declaratory Act declaring the unilateral right of Parliament to pass laws binding on America; the Townshend Revenue Acts imposing taxes on many commonly used products including tea; the Boston Port Act closing the port of Boston to all commerce; the Quebec Act expanding the boundary of Canada southward deep into the present-day United States; the Mutiny Act allowing British troops to be quartered in American homes; and the Intolerable Acts that severely curtailed long-standing freedoms of American colonists. In England, the Intolerable Acts were labeled The Coercive Acts, which seemed to perfectly describe the British government's attitude toward the colonies.

The new measures enacted by Parliament and approved by the King had a certain logic, and the King and his Prime Minister were honestly surprised that Americans were so vehemently opposed to these "fair" measures. In Parliament's view, the colonies should have been glad, even eager, to help pay for the costs of the French and Indian War, won by the British, which secured the colonies from French designs. They should also have been willing to pay for the cost of their own continuing defense, which required the stationing of at least 20,000 troops in America. To the cry of "No Taxation Without Representation" first raised in 1765 by James Otis, a brilliant and inspiring (though increasingly erratic) Boston lawyer, the British responded that Americans were in fact represented in England just as Englishmen all over the world were—by the members of Parliament who looked after the interests of everyone in the Empire. This was called "virtual representation." Moreover, leaders in Britain insisted the taxes were "easy" and definitely not burdensome. Finally, the British firmly held that the colonists were subjects of the King, as were all those under the British flag, and consequently had no right to oppose Parliament's laws that he approved. The King himself was irreversibly set on these laws being enforced without dissent.

The barrage of acts, then, had as their ultimate purpose a substantial increase in tax revenues to be paid by the colonists to help pay for England's debts resulting from the French and Indian War and to shore up the defense of the colonies from further Indian, French, and Spanish incursions. Of course, to the skeptical colonists, there was no assurance the revenues would be used for these purposes. The laws were also intended to severely restrict, primarily to benefit

English commercial interests, colonial business dealings with other nations.

Perhaps of greatest importance, the Intolerable Acts, as noted, frontally attacked basic freedoms—such as the right to assemble and hold meetings and to control the judiciary—and sought in the final analysis to eliminate colonial self-government altogether. Britain considered The Intolerable Acts (which we have seen were labeled The Coercive Acts in England) essential to force or coerce Americans into heeding British tax laws. But to Americans, the Intolerable Acts were the last straw—and they started to realize that England meant to deprive them of all freedom in order to achieve what Parliament and the King wanted.

War on the Horizon

Throughout America in early 1775, colonists, under the guidance of patriot leaders, were beginning to gather gunpowder and weapons in anticipation of British intent to subdue the American population by force. It was becoming increasingly apparent to patriot leaders that the King, George III, in order to obtain the revenues he sought, might very well use military force to compel absolute and unconditional obedience to the will of Parliament and his decrees. The British government was well aware of the colonists' military preparations and was intent on preventing them or capturing or destroying any stored materials of military value.

Consequently, for some time before April 19, 1775, the British had been planning to send a military expedition from Boston to destroy military supplies of the "provincials" in Concord, approximately eighteen miles west of Boston. This was not to be their first mission outside of Boston looking for gunpowder and other military stores, but it would be the farthest march inland. As it was to begin as a night-time raid by a strong infantry force and spearheaded, without protection on its flanks, deep into the rebellious American countryside, it could be seen as a very aggressive and daring move by General Gage.

Paul Revere in Boston

During April, General Gage was under orders from England to arrest Sam Adams and John Hancock, whom British officials in London considered to be ringleaders of the "rebellion" in Massachusetts. The secrecy of the plan—to arrest Hancock and Adams but also to seize or destroy the military supplies and gunpowder at Concord and other towns—was not well-kept by the British military authorities and consequently was known to many Boston citizens. The exact time and manner of the British mission, however, was not known.

Only two days before, on Sunday, April 16, 1775, Paul Revere—a skilled silversmith by occupation and a respected and reliable courier for the Boston patriots, highly active in patriot resistance—had been dispatched to Lexington. His purpose was to warn Adams and Hancock that the British were mobilizing, although the date and timing of their actual departure from Boston to the mainland was yet to be determined. This ride on Sunday, April 16, was Revere's second to Lexington. Little more than a week before, on Saturday, April 8, he had ridden to Lexington, warning Adams and Hancock the British were then about to march. This April 8 warning, however, turned out to be a false alarm.

Statue of Paul Revere in Boston near The Old North Church

Paul Revere had become increasingly worried his rides warning about British intentions might be thwarted. He was "apprehensive" that, at the very point in time when the British Regulars actually did move out from Boston to invade the Massachusetts countryside, he might be captured or prevented from delivering this critical news before he could get to Charlestown across the Charles River. Charlestown was the first stop on his intended route to Lexington. Even if he or other couriers from Boston were captured, he still wanted the patriots in Charlestown to know that the Regulars were moving out and in which direction. He wanted to be certain that, no matter what happened, the invasion alert would be carried, via the patriots in Charlestown, to Lexington and Concord and other Massachusetts towns.

As a result of Revere's concern, on Sunday, April 16, during his return to Boston from his second ride to Lexington, he arranged a back-up plan with patriot and militia leaders in Charlestown. They all agreed that the steeple of Boston's Old North Church would be used for lantern signals.

The Old North Church

The Old North Church was an architectural masterpiece of that period (and it still is today) due to its height, English-based design with expensive brickwork, bells, an ornate clock, chandeliers and organ. It was the highest structure in the city, the top of its sharp steeple rising 191 feet. An Anglican church, also known as Christ's Church, with several "Loyalist members," it was close to the north shore of Boston and directly across from Charlestown, less than a half mile from the Charlestown wharf. The lanterns hung in the steeple would signal when and how the British Regulars would be starting their march into Massachusetts: Two lighted lanterns would be hung if the Regulars were then crossing the Charles River (or Back Bay) by boat, while just one lantern would be displayed if the British intrusion into the countryside was occurring by land via the Boston Neck. This "land or sea" information was very important because the Boston Neck land route to Lexington and Concord was considerably longer in time and in distance. The "land" route also used a different road on the mainland, starting out, than the road that would be used if the Charles River was the route chosen by the British.

Old North Church. On the night of April 18, 1775, Paul Revere directed two lanterns be hung in the steeple of this church to signal that the Regulars were starting their march into the Massachusetts countryside "by sea"—crossing the Charles River.

It also seems very likely that Paul Revere knew on April 16, and had discussed with the militia leaders in Charlestown, that the British military expedition from Boston was imminent and would take place at night. As we have seen, it was Revere's intent that the lantern signals would be displayed whether or not he was able to escape Boston for his warning ride—so that no matter what happened, the British actions would be immediately known to patriots outside of the city.

Assignment: Lexington

Two days later, at about 9:00 in the evening on Tuesday, April 18, Dr. Joseph Warren, an accomplished physician and surgeon and the last remaining patriot leader in Boston, learned with certainty that the British Regulars would be moving out that night (Dr. Warren was to lose his life two months later fighting in the Battle of Bunker Hill).

Dr. Warren had been informed by a confidential source that the British were using a combat-trained force of 1,200 to 1,500 Regulars (this intelligence overestimated the number of troops)—a combination of light infantry, noted for their agility and tactics, and "grenadiers," known for their exceptional strength and size (a grenadier had to be at least six feet tall). The troops would be crossing the Back Bay in longboats with the intent of landing on a point on shore, called Lechmere's Point, on the north end of the marshland just west of Charlestown. The confidential source for this information was probably Margaret Kemble Gage, the attractive American wife of the British General Gage. She was known to have strong sympathy for the patriots' cause.

As soon as he received this intelligence, Dr. Warren sent an urgent message to his friend and confidant, Paul Revere, who came immediately from his home to find out "what was acting" (one of his favorite expressions). Dr. Warren gave him the news about 10:00 p.m. that the British Regulars were, at that very hour, moving from their barracks west across the Boston Common to their embarkation boats on the southwest shore of Boston. Revere, who had noticed the British movements that evening himself, was further told that the intent of the expedition was to arrest Sam Adams and John Hancock (who were known by virtue of British spies to be in Lexington) or to destroy provincial military supplies at Concord. As it turned out, the actual written orders that General Gage gave to the officer commanding the British force only directed the objective of destroying the military stores at Concord.

Revere was assigned the task of leaving at once to warn Adams and Hancock in Lexington. Another messenger, William Dawes, had already left—using a different route to get to Lexington, the Boston Neck. (Dr. Warren left no room for error—and both messengers eventually reached Lexington—Paul Revere arriving first. A third messenger may also have been sent.) Both routes to Lexington were hazardous because of British guards and armed patrols posted and riding between various points on the road to Lexington and Concord.

One if by land and two if by sea
And I on the opposite shore will be

—Henry Wadsworth Longfellow, Paul Revere's Ride

Two Lanterns

As soon as he received this assignment from Dr. Warren, Revere headed home to get his riding boots, which he had apparently forgotten. On the way to his North Boston house (which still exists today), he stopped and directed friends and fellow patriots, with whom he had previously discussed his plans, to hang two lanterns in the steeple of the Old North Church—the pre-arranged signal to the patriots in Charlestown that the British Regulars were then leaving Boston by water. After getting his boots, he hurried to the banks of the Charles River on the north side of Boston.

It must be remembered that Boston was forcibly occupied by British forces and, along with a curfew, all citizen activity was closely scrutinized by the authorities. So it was with great suspense, difficulty, and courage that two lighted lanterns were hung, by Revere's friends (Robert Newman, John Pulling, and Thomas Bernard), a little after 10:00 p.m. in the steeple of the Old North Church—two lights gleaming high in the dark night sky for just a few moments. With the help of two more friends, Joshua Bentley and Thomas Richardson, at about 10:30 on that Tuesday night and before the British force finished embarking on their longboats, Revere himself successfully made it over the Charles River. He used a small rowboat, his own boat, which he had hidden beforehand on the bank of the river.

Photo of The Old North Church as it stands today in Boston. It still towers over other structures in Boston's historic North End. Across the water in Is Charlestown

With a full moon over the horizon and high tide just beginning, Paul Revere crossed the Charles River in the rising moon's glare and changing shadows, right under the noses of several British warships anchored there, including the massive, shifting, and creaking man-of-war "HMS *Somerset*", armed with sixty-four cannons. "HMS" stands for His Majesty's Ship," an ironic historical fact given that Revere was, at that very place and hour, starting his dash to gain America's freedom from the British monarch. Landing on the Charlestown side, he made his way into town, where he met members of the Charlestown militia and their leader, Colonel William Conant. Revere told them "what was acting"—explaining more details about the British march.

The militia in Charlestown had seen the lantern signals and had already sent out a rider to the nearby countryside and to Lexington with the news. The fate of this messenger was never learned, though he may have been captured by one of the British patrols because he never made it to Lexington. Revere then went to "git me a horse." While the horse was being saddled for the ride, Richard Devens of the Charlestown Committee of Safety (a patriot citizen group that carried out paramilitary and police activities) approached Revere and told him that armed British officers, "mounted on good horses," were patrolling the road to Lexington. Devens said he personally had encountered a party of nine or ten British officers earlier that evening headed in the direction of Concord.

The Road to Lexington

For, borne on the night-wind of the past,
Through all our history, to the last,
In the hour of darkness and peril and need,
The people will waken and listen to hear
The hurrying hoofbeats of that steed,
And the midnight message of Paul Revere.

—Henry Wadsworth Longfellow, "Paul Revere's Ride"

For the mission to Lexington, Revere borrowed a "very good horse," fast and reliable, owned by Deacon John Larkin of Charlestown. Some accounts say the horse's name was Brown Beauty. An expert horseman, Revere had no difficulty mounting and controlling the large and powerful Brown Beauty—and, with a firm grip on the reins and disregarding the warnings about armed British patrols, he turned at once toward the road to Lexington. It was about 11:00 p.m. and it would be a twelve-mile, one-hour ride in darkness. As this was his third trip to Lexington in the last two weeks and the full moon was now high in the clear sky, he had no problems navigating the journey.

Early on, however, after crossing the "Charlestown Neck" leading to the adjacent town of Cambridge, he was forced to make a skillful galloping detour to the north—lengthening his trip by several minutes—to avoid being captured by a pursuing two-man armed British patrol that had been lurking in the moon-shadows of trees alongside the road! The speed and strength of Brown Beauty clearly helped him successfully escape the patrol.

After eluding the British officers, Revere, at high but controlled speed, continued with his ride—finding the weather, as he later reported, to be "very pleasant' and the moon "shone bright." In this famous and legendary but totally true "midnight ride" to Lexington, Paul Revere carried the written message from Dr. Warren to Sam Adams and John Hancock that a large force of British Regulars had crossed the Charles River and were on the march to arrest them—and that the military supplies at Concord were also a likely target. Revere fully grasped the importance of his mission and had no intention of allowing anyone to stop him.

Upon reaching the town of Mystic (present-day Medford), about three miles northwest of Cambridge, Revere awoke and alerted the Minutemen Captain there. Then, galloping westward, he gave the alarm, probably by knocking on doors and windows, to almost every house along the road to Lexington that the "Regulars were out."

About midnight, pulling back hard on the reins of heavily breathing Brown Beauty, whose hooves were pounding deep into the wet, dirt road, Paul Revere came to a jarring halt directly in front of Rev. Clarke's parsonage in Lexington. It was guarded by ten members of the Lexington militia. The sergeant in command of the small unit, William Munroe, sternly warned Revere to be quiet. Not heeding this warning and telling the sergeant "the Regulars are out!", Revere immediately dismounted and, loudly knocking on the door of the house, delivered his urgent message to the already-awake patriot leaders, Adams and Hancock (they had opened a window to see what was going on). Both of them knew Revere very well and trusted him completely. Within a few minutes of Revere's arrival, the warning went out to the Lexington militia captain, who lived two miles away. William Dawes, the second messenger from Boston, came on the scene thirty minutes after Revere, confirming the news from Boston that the Regulars were on the march.

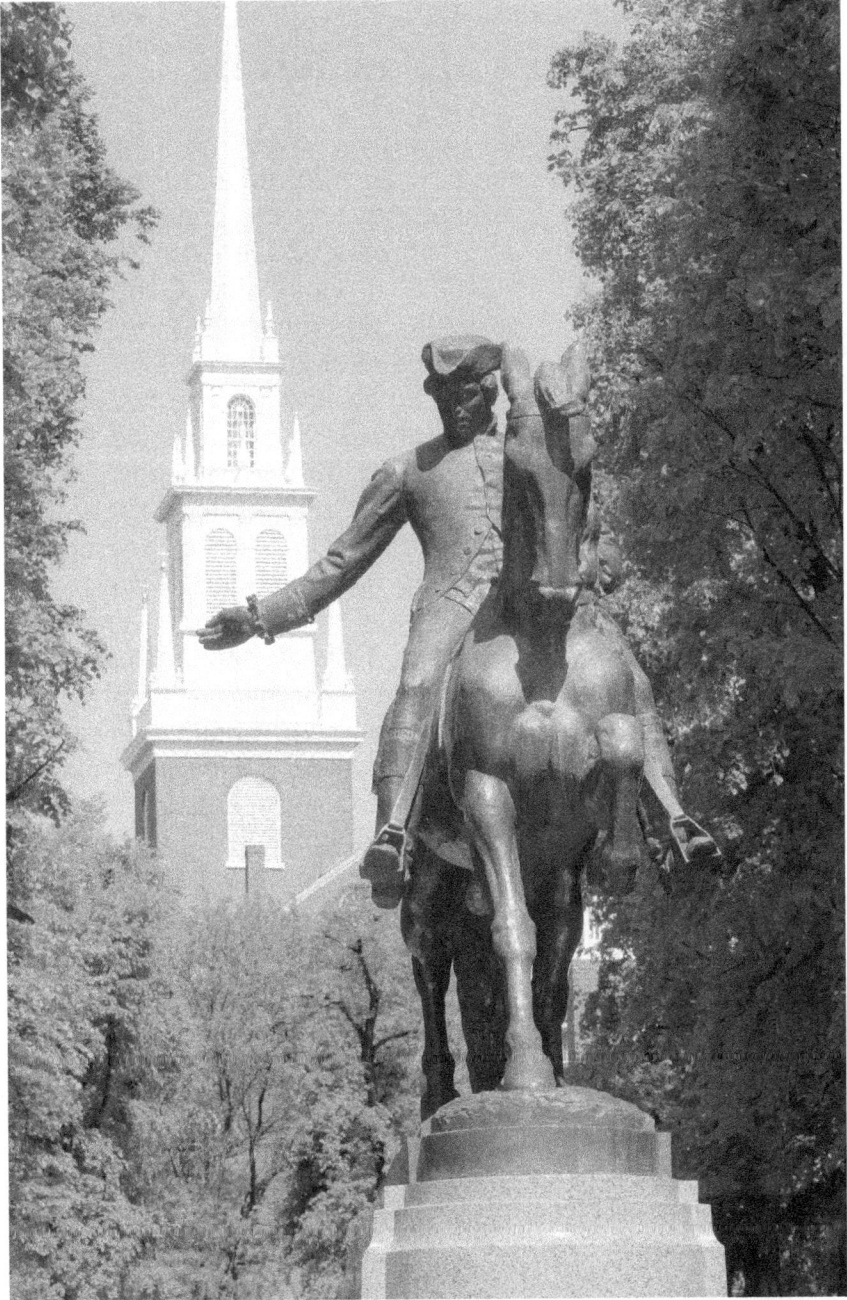

*Statue of Paul Revere (as it stands near The Old North Church today)
alerting the Massachusetts countryside*

Capture of Paul Revere

Arresting Sam Adams and John Hancock had long been a British objective. However, both Dr. Warren and Paul Revere and other patriot leaders knew (due to the intelligence they had received and the large force that General Gage was using—it turned out to be 850 troops), that Gage's likely main goal that night was the destruction of the military supplies at Concord, six miles west of Lexington.

So, after stopping at Lexington and alerting the patriots and militia and taking a rest and getting something to eat, about 1:30 or 2:00 a.m. on April 19, Revere and Dawes remounted and galloped toward Concord to deliver their warning. But only one messenger, Dr. Samuel Prescott of Concord, who had been visiting his fiancé in Lexington and joined Dawes and Revere just outside of Lexington, eventually made it to Concord. Revere himself, unarmed, was captured a short time later by another patrol of British officers on horseback when he was about halfway to Concord. Dawes and Prescott narrowly escaped capture. Dawes lost his horse and was unable to continue. Prescott continued on horseback to Concord and alerted the minutemen there that the Regulars were out in force and heading for Concord.

Because guarding a prisoner interfered with their patrol duties, after about an hour the British officers, who had learned Revere's identity and were well aware of his importance, reluctantly released him very near Lexington (but without Brown Beauty, which they commandeered for a sergeant of British Grenadiers, who had a "small, tired out horse"). Before his release, Revere, a pistol pointed at his head and threatened with his brains being "blown out," told the officers that he knew the British plans, the entire countryside was alerted, and that "500 Americans" would be waiting for the Regulars in Lexington. The number "500" was exaggerated, but this was not intentional. Revere had assumed that, because of the warning he gave to every house on his ride to Lexington, probably at least that many men would be waiting in town. And he was apparently hoping the information about American strength would deter the British plans. But he was mistaken. Alarmed by the information they had learned, the British officers, after letting Revere go (within sight of the Lexington meetinghouse), galloped back to the main British force. There they personally reported this new intelligence to the officer leading the advance detachment of infantry. The column was by that time, now after 4:00 a.m., fast approaching the eastern outskirts of Lexington.

At the same time, Paul Revere, just released by the British officers, quickly returned on foot to the Lexington Common (passing through the Lexington "burial ground")— to tell the story of his capture and the information he had learned. He probably got to Lexington near 4:30 a.m. While in Lexington, he spent a few minutes to help Hancock and Adams make a delayed and hurried escape, by way of a carriage, to a parsonage close to the nearby town of Woburn. After briefly helping with this escape, Revere then returned to the Lexington Common. He probably was there about 4:45 or 4:50 a.m. There, in another act of on-the-spot courage and quick-thinking, he helped "rescue," in the nick of time, a heavy trunk of John Hancock's papers that had been stored for safekeeping in, of all places, the attic of the Buckman Tavern next to the Common! (These papers, if they had been recovered by the British Regulars, probably would have given them absolute proof of Hancock's "treason.")

As for the marching Regulars, their commanding officer, Colonel Francis Smith, on receiving the new intelligence (that had originated with Paul Revere) from the British patrol, sent a dispatch back to General Gage in Boston for reinforcements. The British troops then quickened the march to Concord. The intended route of their expedition went directly through Lexington and its Common.

Chapter Three

The Common

A Green Triangle

The Lexington Common today is a triangle of lawn, bordered by busy Lexington streets, with the east point of the triangle facing the road going toward Boston. On the opposite side, or base of the triangle, one point looks west toward the road to Concord and the other point northwest toward Bedford. The triangle is not a very large or expansive area. Except for the monuments and some preserved buildings including the adjacent wooden tavern, the Buckman Tavern, where some militia had waited on the night of April 18-19, 1775, there is nothing there today to hint that it is a historic battlefield that marked the beginning of American independence.

In 1775, the triangle was approximately 600 feet long from east to west. The town's Congregational Church (its only church), pastored by Rev. Jonas Clarke and called the meetinghouse, was located in the vortex of the east point of the Common (this meetinghouse is no longer there). The west-northwest base of the triangle in 1775 was about 400 feet long. The terrain of the triangle probably was irregular and considerably rougher in 1775 than today. It was to this triangle of grass, the Common, also known as the "parade," that the Lexington militia was ordered by battle drums and alarm guns at 1:00 a.m. on April 19, 1775, in response to the midnight alert brought by Paul Revere and others.

The Lexington Militia

There were 146 men (almost all of the able-bodied men in town) in the Lexington militia, better known then as the "Lexington Training Band." Many were farmers, mostly dairy farmers. Others were mechanics, tradesmen, and apprentices. All were volunteers (but were expected to serve), probably paid one shilling for each day of active service. In very approximate terms, a shilling (1/20th of a British pound) was then worth about forty to fifty dollars in 2012 terms. Not all the militia were adult men—more than 10 percent were teenage boys ranging from age sixteen to nineteen. At least nine of the men were over fifty, with several over sixty. One of the militia was an African American slave with the interesting name of Prince Estabrook.

In those times, it seems that a part of each militia force or training band in New England was to be composed of "minutemen." Following this practice, the Massachusetts Provincial Congress (considered an illegal colonial body by the British) had recommended in early 1775 that one-quarter of every town's militia be designated as minutemen—to be ready at a moment's notice when alerted for duty. But apparently there is no definite record that the town of Lexington actually specified a percentage of militia for the minuteman role as most other towns did. Nonetheless, that morning it appears the entire Lexington militia was expected to be ready at a "moment's notice."

On that particular day, then, all of them were "minutemen" in the practical sense of that word, even if not officially designated as such. It also seems that men over fifty as well as teenage boys were intended to be part of an "alarm list" (rather than being in the first line militia). They would be called for combat duty only if absolutely necessary. Be that as it may, at 1:00 a.m. that morning, at the roll of the battle drums, all of them, young and old, were "minutemen," summoned by their captain to report immediately to the Common to "consult what to do."

Captain Parker

Captain John Parker, the militia leader in Lexington, was a forty-six-year-old farmer, married with seven children, and a veteran of the French and Indian War. He was a member of the Lexington Congregational Church (as were most others in town) and well-respected by the militia, which displayed its confidence by electing him captain of their company. Although a strong, discerning, and able man, he was not in good health, suffering from tuberculosis from which he was to die about five months later. But neither his farm, nor his worsening health, nor his family responsibilities interfered with his willingness to lead the militia.

Chapter Four

America's Sunrise

They were determined to stand by their rights to the last.

—Rev. Jonas Clarke

The names of Munroe, Parker and others that fell...shall be held in grateful remembrance by the people of this land and transmitted to posterity, with honor and respect, throughout all generations.

—Rev. Jonas Clarke

they went where duty seemed to call

—John Greenleaf Whittier

Call to the Common

It is not known with certainty today exactly how many of the Lexington militia came to the Common when Captain Parker ordered the company's teenage drummer, William Diamond, to summon them at 1:00 a.m. on April 19, 1775. Lexington is a "spread out" town, so they had to come from varying distances, some from several miles, and it is possible not everyone heard the alarm. Having been alerted earlier to the presence of British patrols, some may already have been in town near the Common, probably gathered and keeping warm in the Buckman Tavern next to it (the tavern was and

The Buckman Tavern as restored today (author in front). Some of the Lexington minutemen gathered here in the early hours of April 19, 1775.

is furnished with an extra-wide and unusually high fireplace suitable for a large blazing fire, which can still be seen today). In any event, although the exact number of militia responding to the alarm is unknown, there is reason to believe that almost all of the company of 146 was mustered and present for duty, shouldering their muskets, by no later than 2:00 a.m.

Because of the information brought by Paul Revere, Captain Parker apparently was under the impression the British force had left the Charlestown area around 11:30 p.m. or midnight. This would indicate that the marching Regulars would arrive in Lexington about 3:00 a.m. or even earlier. Paul Revere evidently had some information about the British delay in the Cambridge marshes and had probably reported that to Captain Parker. But it seems quite likely the militia captain was not, at 1:00 a.m., aware of the full extent of the various British operational problems—insufficient and inadequate boats in crossing the Back Bay, missing their objective of Lechmere's Point, and getting bogged down in the soft Cambridge marshland, all of which delayed their march about two hours.

Dismissal at 3:00 a.m.

But Captain Parker was a careful military leader and sent out his own scouts to locate the British force. One of these scouts returned close to 3:00 a.m. and told Parker that no British troops were seen on the road from Cambridge. Upon receiving this report (which turned out to be gravely mistaken) and not being sure of the British location and probably also beginning to have some doubt they were actually coming, Captain Parker dismissed his men, probably between 3:00 and 3:30 a.m. But, not taking any chances, he gave them orders to stay near the town and to return immediately upon hearing the beat of the drums.

Before the men were dismissed, it had been decided after a meeting, and the order was given by Captain Parker, that the militia would not interfere or "meddle" with the Regulars nor even be seen ("not to be discovered") unless the British force "insulted" them. Captain Parker stayed on or near the Common in those early hours of April 19. It also appears that, between approximately 2:00 and 3:00 a.m., the company of militia was briefly visited by Sam Adams and John Hancock—and also by Rev. Clarke, who most likely said a prayer, as would be the custom for town ministers at that time.

"They Are Here!"

Then, at about 4:25 a.m., in a heart-gripping, breathless instant of enduring historic importance, the last of Captain Parker's scouts, Thaddeus Bowman, galloped onto the Common at full speed. Shattering the stillness of that sleepy hour, he was hollering at the top of his lungs that a large force of Regulars was just a short distance away, "past the rocks"—less than two miles from the Common! Paul Revere had been right all along—they were out!

Captain Parker immediately ordered the battle roll of the drums and alarm guns fired to recall the militia—and he and the other officers of the company then anxiously waited for them to return. After several minutes, as men and teenage boys were running back to the Common individually and in small groups, a mass of British Regulars suddenly appeared in the distance, about a quarter mile toward the east, on the road that turned toward the Common. The sun behind them was straining to rise; sunrise was at 4:57 a.m.

Facing the Regulars

The King's Troops, a unit of 240 light infantry, were dangerously close. This advance British contingent, red-coated and armed with long brown muskets nearly five feet long, sharpened bayonets attached, appeared to the militia to be a much larger force than 240. Some yards behind them, not yet in sight, was the remaining force of about 600 Regulars. In disciplined, menacing, military columns filling the road, the frontline Redcoats, in lockstep, were striding quickly and with fierce determination in the direction of the meetinghouse on the east side of the Common.

We were faced toward the Regulars.

—Sworn statement of fourteen Lexington militia

Damn them, we will have them!

—British officer as reported by Rev. Jonas Clarke

As the Lexington militia came running onto the Common, they were ordered to form two rows near the northwest side (toward Bedford) of the triangle, facing the meetinghouse and the marching Regulars, but not blocking the road to Concord. Looking east, they also faced the light of the approaching dawn. They had not yet fully mustered— only about forty to sixty men were organized, while still others, perhaps about twenty, some with their backs to the King's Troops, were just arriving or then on the Common (later reports indicate a total of seventy-seven militia were on the green when the shooting started).

Although not in the militia, Paul Revere was present on the Common, very close to the two rows of the militia company—and he distinctly heard Captain Parker say, "Let the troops pass by and don't molest them without they begin first."

No Brighter Dawn

And this is the place where the fatal scene begins! They approach with the morning light.

—Rev. Jonas Clarke

Sunrise as it may have looked on April 19, 1775

Just as the militia was organizing into its two rows and as the piercing golden brilliance of the still-hidden sun, appearing now as an orange-reddish glow through the budding distant trees, was about to break free of the eastern horizon, a mounted British officer, Major John Pitcairn, galloped around the side of the meetinghouse. His bright scarlet officer's jacket was visible and he was brandishing a sword in his right hand. He approached very quickly to within about 100 feet of the small militia company, who clearly saw him and the troops behind him. Waving the sword high in the air in a threatening manner, his horse strutting and rearing, Major Pitcairn was shouting, excitedly, very loudly, and forcefully, "DISPERSE YOU REBELS—DAMN YOU, THROW DOWN YOUR ARMS AND DISPERSE!"

Behind this officer were two other mounted officers also shouting and threatening the militia. And behind them were the fast-marching infantry, carrying their muskets primed and loaded, with the ominous bayonets visible under the brightening sky. The Regulars could see the tiny band of militia standing straight, with their muskets, on the far side of the Common, and they also saw other men and boys running toward it.

Submission to the King

Hearing the British officer's demands and quickly glancing at the fast-approaching, overwhelmingly massive force of the best infantry in the world, Captain Parker gave the order for his men to disperse. (Some eyewitness accounts indicate Captain Parker, perhaps to avoid provoking an attack, ordered his men to disperse just before the British officer shouted his demands.) Most of them began to comply, many doing so with their backs turned toward the Regulars. As the militia started to disperse, none ran and some moved slowly. A very few, apparently not hearing the order, did not move at all. No one dropped his musket. While this was happening, the British infantry, marching quickly around both sides of the meetinghouse, were shouting their deafening battle cry—"HUZZA, HUZZA, HUZZA"—which must have sounded like gigantic swarms of angry hornets to Captain Parker and the dispersing militia.

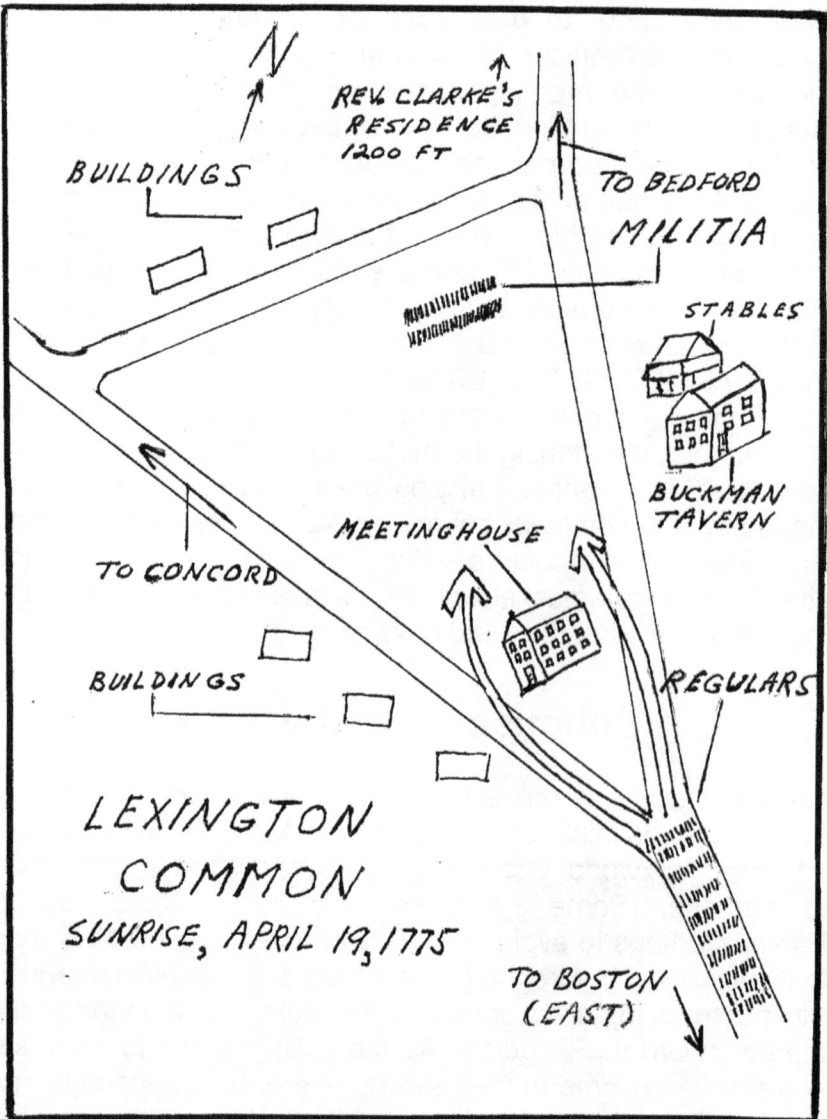

BUILDINGS

REV. CLARKE'S
RESIDENCE
1200 FT

TO BEDFORD

MILITIA

STABLES

BUCKMAN
TAVERN

TO CONCORD

MEETINGHOUSE

BUILDINGS

REGULARS

LEXINGTON
COMMON
SUNRISE, APRIL 19, 1775

TO BOSTON
(EAST)

Sketch by author of Lexington Common at sunrise, April 19, 1775

The First Shot

Engraving of the Battle of Lexington

Fire! By God, Fire!

—orders of British officer (probably Major Pitcairn) as
reported by Rev. Jonas Clarke

According to the sworn statements of eyewitnesses,
including a captured British soldier who was in the ranks of
the light infantry, just as the Lexington militia was dispersing,
a British officer fired a pistol in their direction. Then, as the
sun was beginning its inevitable rise, and as recounted by
eyewitnesses, the British officer in the forefront ordered the
infantry to fire.

In their reports of the battle, British officers emphatically
denied they gave any order to fire or that they were
responsible for the first shot. They said the first shot came
from one of the nearby buildings, from the meetinghouse, or
from the direction of a stone wall next to the Common.
Historians have used these reports and similar information to
conclude that someone fired the first shot but no one knows
for sure who it was. But as noted, several eyewitness
accounts, including statements of many of the militia
present, given in their sworn statements within a week of the
battle, reported the events very differently—that the
Regulars fired first. At least three witnesses testified they
heard the leading British officer give the order to fire. These
various statements, made under oath, being so near in time
to the event and consistent in their basic facts, have the ring
of truth. Moreover, it would also seem almost impossible that
highly trained British Regulars would fire without orders from
their officers. In fact they had been ordered not to fire without
receiving orders. All accounts agree that the Lexington militia
on the Common facing the British did not fire first.

The most convincing evidence that the first shot was
fired by the Regulars comes from none other than Paul
Revere. In his own deposition prepared for the
Massachusetts Provincial Congress made soon after the
battle, he specifically reported hearing the first shot. Still
near the Common, he said he had turned his head after he

heard the shot and saw the smoke from that shot in front of the British troops. This statement by the trustworthy Revere is consistent with other reports, given by several witnesses, that one of the British officers in front of the infantry had fired his pistol, and that with this shot the battle had begun.

After this, the Regulars rushed forward, again with a great shout. Briefly pausing to level their weapons, several of them fired in scattered volleys, then all in regular volleys, a tremendous withering blast of musketry.

Re-enactment of attacking British Regulars

Jonas Parker Fights Back

Unquestionably, the beginning British musket fire occurred while the militia was dispersing and before any of them fired—and only a few, maybe eight, were able to fire back after the Regulars had fired. One who fought back was Jonas Parker. He was in his fifties, a cousin of Captain Parker and probably on the "alarm list." He had not moved from his position on the green. Before getting off his first shot, he was hit by the fire of the Regulars and knocked to the ground. Kneeling or lying there and facing the British, Jonas Parker fired into the drifting smoke of their volleys. Then, attempting to reload his musket while on the ground, he felt the powerful and fatal sting of a bayonet as the Regulars rushed over the Common.

Those Who Fell For Their Country

But they bleed, they die, not in their own cause only, but in the cause of this whole people—in the cause of God, their country and posterity.

—Rev. Jonas Clarke

In the attack, eight of the militia were killed almost instantly and ten were wounded by the Regulars' volleys. Many were hit in the back as they were dispersing or running from the repeated musket fire. Those who died for their country at that sunrise were John Brown, Samuel Hadley, Caleb Harrington, Jonathan Harrington, Jr., Robert Munroe, Isaac Muzzy, Jonas Parker, and Asahel Porter (who lived in Woburn). The oldest killed was sixty-two; the youngest probably in his twenties. Prince Estabrook, the black slave, was among the wounded (he would fight again in the War and gain his freedom.) The others wounded in that morning battle were Jacob Bacon (from the town of Woburn), John Robbins, Solomon Pierce, John Tidd, Joseph Comee, Ebenezer Munroe, Jr., Thomas Winship, Nathaniel Farmer, and Jedediah Munroe. Captain Parker was not hit. One of the wounded, Jedediah Munroe, fifty-four, was killed later in the day along with two other Lexington militia, John Raymonds and Nathaniel Wyman, while fighting on "Battle Road" that marked the British retreat from Concord. It seems only one or two of the British troops and one of their horses suffered slight wounds.

After their first volley, the British infantry reloaded (they were able to do this very quickly, perhaps in fifteen seconds) and fired again and again—Jonas Parker apparently was hit in the second volley. After several long, terrible moments of heavy musket firing and as rays of sunlight began to flood the Common, all signs of the militia, except for the dead lying on the grass wet with dew, disappeared from the sight of the British. The commanding officer of the entire British expedition, Colonel Francis Smith, then was on the scene.

The King's Troops "proceeded in warlike array to Concord."

—Thomas Jefferson and John Dickinson

Seeing there was no further resistance, the stunned but clear-thinking and experienced Colonel Smith, using his drummers, ordered the firing to stop. After several minutes he was able to reorganize his highly excited men, who were almost totally out of control. After restoring order, he allowed them to shout three tumultuous cheers and to fire a massive victory volley, hundreds of musket explosions echoing for miles into the countryside. With the long morning shadow of the meetinghouse now cast over the Common where the minutemen had fallen, Colonel Smith ordered the 850 Regulars, re-formed into their combat-ready columns, to continue their march through Lexington directly to Concord six miles ahead.

Concord

Fire fellow soldiers! For God's sake, fire!

—Major John Buttrick, Concord Militia, after being fired upon by the British Regulars at the North Bridge in Concord

The Regulars reached Concord without opposition about 7:30 a.m. As they approached and entered the village in military formation, they were closely observed, from high ground north of the road, by the alerted and waiting town militia. Elements of the British force were ordered to search outlying homes and farms for "military stores." But the Regulars were confronted and repulsed, about a mile past the center of town, at the "Old North Bridge" over the Concord River. To the surprise of the British, several hundred minutemen from militia companies in Concord and from many other Massachusetts (and New Hampshire) towns were on the scene.

Hearing the early alarm, many minutemen had actually run several miles, through fields and creeks and over hills and fences, all the way to Concord. Organized on a gradually inclining grassy hillside, under the command of Colonel James Barrett and Major John Buttrick, about 200 yards from the bridge, the minutemen, as in Lexington, were ordered not to fire first and did not fire first at the King's Troops. A company of Regulars was the first to fire as the minutemen marched down the hillside toward the bridge with the intent of retaking the bridge (which the British company had started to dismantle) and forcing the Regulars from the town where they had set fires.

Despite two minutemen in the frontline of the Americans, Captain Isaac Davis and Private Abner Hosmer, both from the town of Acton, being instantly killed by the opening British volley, the Americans' return musket fire was accurate and effective, causing heavy British casualties. This battle at Concord's North Bridge in fact started the eventual British retreat. It was in his poem "Concord Hymn," written sixty-one years later, that Ralph Waldo Emerson referred to the minutemen's return musket fire, ordered by Major Buttrick, as "the shot heard round the world." While in Concord and before the Regulars started their retreat to Boston, two Concord physicians treated several wounded British officers, as if to let them know that the American "rebels" were not as bad as they had been painted.

Concord's Old North Bridge as reconstructed today

The "grassy hillside" looking down on Concord's Old North Bridge

After several hours spent searching Concord and its outlying areas for "provincial military stores," the frustrated Regulars, suffering from the losses sustained at the North Bridge, and from fatigue and thirst, were compelled in the early afternoon of April 19 to leave Concord. They set out to return the way they had come, through Lexington, to the safety net of Boston. Their mission to destroy military supplies had been practically fruitless: The alerted colonists had effectively hidden almost all gunpowder, ammunition, and weapons or dispersed them to nearby farms and villages. Nor, of course, had the Regulars captured John Hancock or Sam Adams.

Battle Road

During that afternoon and the early evening of April 19, although receiving reinforcement in the early afternoon of approximately 1,900 Regulars and two artillery pieces dispatched by General Gage, the British retreat from Concord turned into a confused and panic-stricken gauntlet as they fled on a long, winding road to their Boston citadel. Nearly four thousand minutemen and militia, from more than thirty towns and under organized leadership, had with amazing speed converged on the front, rear, and flanks of the Regulars' path, which today is preserved as "Battle Road." Even Dr. Warren, who had sent Paul Revere on his mission the previous night, came out from Boston and fought in the battle late that afternoon.

The combat on Battle Road frequently was very violent—and painful and deadly, especially for the Regulars. Though fighting bravely and sometimes brutally (killing some captives), they were low on ammunition, now outnumbered and, in their red coats, easy targets for the sharpshooting minutemen. The British were desperate to get back to Boston. To find or root out minutemen snipers and destroy hiding places, the angry Regulars set fire to and ransacked several homes, barns, and shops along their wild retreat.

When the night shadows ended that historic day of April 19, 1775, the exhausted Regulars, finally reaching their Boston haven in a cold rain, frustrated and hurting, had suffered a serious and unexpected defeat. The main force of the King's Troops had marched well over thirty-six miles carrying heavy muskets and other gear and were frequent targets of incessant gunfire. They had sustained severe casualties, most caused by the attacks during their retreat along the narrow, blood-stained miles of Battle Road—attacks by well-led minutemen from ambush and from behind stone fences, barns, houses, and trees. Some of the British later complained that this form of warfare was uncivilized.

Although accounts of the battle results that day differ in minor respects, British casualties for the entire mission appear to have been 73 killed, 174 wounded, and 25 missing (probably all captured). American casualties for the day, including non-militia, were 49 killed and 39 wounded. The Lexington militia suffered 20 percent of those killed. The British number of wounded was probably much higher since they, stoically, only counted extremely serious injuries as wounds.

An important military result of the defeat was that all British troops had been forced into their confined Boston stronghold where, to their astonishment, they found themselves surrounded by thousands of armed Americans from all over New England. Following the Battle of Bunker Hill two months later (June 1775), they remained isolated and besieged in Boston for eight more months. They were eventually forced by American military forces (comprised of the newly formed Continental Army under General George Washington) to evacuate Boston by sea in March 1776.

George Washington. He skillfully led the new American Continental Army in driving the British from Boston in March 1776. New England minutemen companies were included in his army.

Part II

Virtues and Values from that Time

Chapter Five

Admirable Courage

**No berserk thirst of blood had they
No battle joy was theirs…
Their feet had trodden peaceful ways
They loved not strife, they dreaded pain**

—John Greenleaf Whittier

The First Virtue

Probably the first virtue prevalent at this sunrise, certainly evident to anyone reading about the battle, was admirable courage. This was exemplified when:

- Paul Revere crossed the Charles River in danger of British warships and when he turned Brown Beauty toward Lexington without any hesitation, knowing he would be risking death at the hands of armed British patrols;

- Captain Parker called his men back to the Common at 4:30 in the morning where he stood awaiting the British advance;

- The outnumbered militia, at the second call of the battle drums, ran back to the Common at sunrise, facing directly toward the threatening Regulars;

- Jonas Parker, lying on the Common wounded and trying to reload, was bayoneted;

- Jedediah Munroe, though wounded, returned to the fighting that afternoon and was killed in action;

- The militia, including those wounded, returned to the fight later in the day at the summons of Captain Parker.

Many other intrepid actions were taken by young and old, men and women, that day showing selflessness and firmness in the face of danger.

A Different Kind of Courage

Some things are worth fighting for, some are not.

—unknown

But *courage* can be a misused word—as there are many kinds of courage, and it can be confused with other human traits. For example, some might say it took courage for Nazi SS officers to lead the invasion of Poland, Russia, France, Holland, and all of Europe, or when attacking Allied soldiers on the beaches of Normandy or in the Battle of the Bulge. A criminal, and those who admire him or aspire to be one, may believe it takes courage to rob a well-guarded bank or to burglarize a house that has a guard dog or an alarm system. A reckless driver may believe it takes courage to speed 100 miles an hour on a dark and winding country road with friends inside the car. Some may say it takes courage to enter a ring or cage and fight, barefisted, in professional "ultimate fighting" matches, where almost any kind of wanton, unspeakable brutality, including smashing the battered face of a downed opponent, is allowed.

But foolish behavior, reckless destruction, knowing obedience to evil (that is to say, obedience to a system, power, or set of beliefs recognized as evil by scripture and by most civilized nations), wanton brutality, violent acts intended to injure a fellow human being simply because of hatred or in order to receive money, success, or fame, criminal acts and the like, are not truly courageous and should not be mentioned in the same breath with the courage shown by the minutemen on April 19, 1775.

That courage was admirable and virtuous—those actions and responses, rising from a decent and thoughtful desire to have well-ordered lives and God-given freedom; that protect human liberty from an attacking tyranny; that stand against plainly criminal acts as well as unjustified violence; that protect home, family, community, and country from physical attacks against freedom, life, and democracy; and that advance universally recognized principles of truth, goodness, and peace.

Captain Parker's Courage

while his children were sleeping, rose the bold rebel and shouldered his gun

—Oliver Wendell Holmes

With these thoughts in mind, let's take a closer look at Captain James Parker and consider his probable actions that night. Before learning of General Gage's specific mission from Paul Revere in Lexington, Captain Parker likely had been home with his family and asleep, or trying to sleep, since he had to rise early that spring morning to work his farm. We know he had advanced tuberculosis and was not feeling very well. So it can easily be imagined, at this time in his short life, in his forty-seventh year, that he felt his self-confidence waning and physical strength being tested. Yet near his bed were his musket and his knapsack—perhaps carrying the orders of the Massachusetts Provincial Congress that militia and minutemen should not fire first when facing British Regulars ("act solely on the defensive").

New England dairy farm, perhaps similar to the farm of Captain Parker

After being alerted or awakened by a messenger and collecting his gear silently but swiftly in the dim light of his wide, flickering, New England fireplace, Captain Parker must have cautioned his wife and children, "keep the door locked, don't worry about me, everything will be all right, I will return soon." Then, quickly and with self-confidence that comes from bitter experience and achievement through a life of hard work, and knowing what he was about, he walked silently and intently through the door of his plain Massachusetts farmhouse. He then would have mounted and steadied his horse, perhaps already saddled by one of his older children. Holding the reins firmly and scanning the shadows of the road ahead, he made his way to the Lexington Common, about two miles distant.

Riding to Lexington in the moonlight in those early minutes of April 19, 1775, Captain Parker may have been thinking that the British force marching out from Boston probably had at least 500 troops—as the militia was not to be called out unless an invading British force was at least that size. Knowing that Lexington probably would be on the route of the Regulars, he also was fully aware that his small company of older men, young men, and boys would be greatly outnumbered.

Upon reaching the Common just before 1:00 a.m. and dismounting, we know he immediately ordered the drums to beat and the alarm guns to fire, calling his men to muster on the green. He and his officers then patiently stood waiting for them in the quiet darkness of the cooling air.

By about 2:00 a.m., Captain Parker's militia company had assembled on the Common. He carefully reviewed the men and boys standing before him. He knew each of them well; many were his relatives; all were his friends. Knowing that his military situation was unfavorable to say the least, and that it would be against the orders he was under if he was to initiate any offensive action, Captain Parker then issued his first order, which was given after consulting with his company, who had input in the decision. The militia was "not to be discovered nor to meddle with the Regular Troops (if they should approach) unless they should insult us."

Since he expected the British troops to arrive well before dawn, it seems Captain Parker believed the militia could, with little effort, make themselves "undiscovered" in the darkness of the country town as the Regulars neared. His main purpose, however, was not to engage the Regulars unless they attacked first—in other words, to act only in self-defense and not openly provoke the King's Troops.

But reality often doesn't cooperate with human plans. The Regulars suddenly approached at an unexpected time when the militia was not present—at sunrise! In this moment, with utmost urgency, Captain Parker issued the order to re-assemble his men who, though earlier dismissed at about 3:00 a.m., were to stay nearby. As the ominous loud rumbling of the battle drums and the blasts of the alarm gums again cascaded through the town and over nearby fields, he waited for his company on the Common once more, where they began to arrive and form some minutes before 5:00 a.m. Apparently, since full daylight was fast approaching and concealment was no longer practical, his verbal orders to his company at this moment in time were slightly, but crucially, different from the previous orders. The men were to stand in the open on the Common facing the Regulars but were to let them pass by, and the troops were not be "molested" unless they attacked the militia. In short, the Captain's decision was to not block the British advance nor to hide, but to observe and be seen by the Regulars—and fight only in self-defense, only if fired upon, only if "they start first."

In these actions by Captain Parker we see admirable courage. Of first importance, none of his actions and conduct was aggressive or spurred by malice or hatred. Instead they were planned and taken with only self-defense in mind. Despite his discouraging sickness and likely feelings of inadequacy, he had left the warmth and security of his comfortable farmhouse in the middle of the night. He had gone without delay to the place of danger where he was needed and where he was the leader. And then, in his new order, firmly spoken as the sky was brightening, issued at the moment of crisis, he was willing to openly face the British, but yet not block their aggressive march. Captain Parker's clear intent was to prove to the British officers that, no matter how powerful their force, the militia was not afraid—and were willing to openly stand and defend, if attacked, their town, their freedom, and their families. At that sunrise, there was no time and no longer any willingness to hide!

It is also notable that, when the British officer leading the King's Troops ordered the militia to disperse, Captain Parker was willing to go the second mile and obey the order—knowing he had already made his point that the Americans were not afraid and were ready to fight if necessary. (As we have previously seen, Captain Parker may have given the order to disperse just before the British officer shouted his command.)

At this brief but extremely important moment in American history, when the order to disperse was given, the British had not yet fired—therefore the militia had not been "insulted" and a frontal shooting assault was not expected. An attack in self-defense was not yet called for. Again he showed courage, this time moral courage, by his willingness to submit to the King's officer despite the obvious threat of the oncoming Regulars. Though this act had dire consequences for his men, it in no way denigrates Captain Parker's act of moral courage—which in essence was obedience to an order of the King. By his submission to the British officer, he without question must have thought the Regulars would not attack.

We can conclude, then, that it was physically courageous for Captain Parker to lead the stand on the Common but also courageous, morally, under these circumstances when firing had not yet begun, to give the order to disburse. He and his men were still subjects of the King. At that very critical moment in history, when he gave that order, the American Revolutionary War had not yet begun!

Jonas Parker's Courage

We are resolved to die freemen rather than to live slaves

—Thomas Jefferson and John Dickinson

According to some accounts of the battle, a few of the militia did not hear Captain Parker's order to disperse. One of these must have been Jonas Parker, over fifty years old, who did not move from his position facing the British infantry. (His son, Jonas Parker, Jr., was also in the militia facing the Regulars that morning, but was not hit.) After the ear-shattering blasts of the musketry volleys fired by the Regulars and hearing the whistle of the musket balls, Jonas Parker knew for sure it was all right to fire back because the militia had now, without any doubt, been "insulted."

But then he was hit. It must have been a serious wound because it knocked him to the ground. Yet, while reeling from the shock of his injury, Jonas Parker fired his first shot and even began to re-load his musket, not an easy task lying injured and bleeding on the ground surrounded by the din of battle. Before getting off his second shot, he felt the searing, fatal thrust of a bayonet— and he could resist no more.

This also was admirable courage—standing firmly in the face of an attack on his town, his country, and his freedom. He was fighting, almost alone and without any thought for his own wounds or safety, to stop overwhelming regiments of attacking and shouting troops.

Jedediah Munroe—a Very Special Courage

They were equally determined to stand by their rights to the last

—Rev. Jonas Clarke

Jedediah Munroe's courage was of no lesser value and of very special significance. Wounded in the battle at that sunrise, he later in the morning had time to consider what to do next, time to talk to his family, time to assess the purpose and goals of his life, time to perhaps think he had already done his part and to let "someone else do it," and certainly time to have the manpower and firepower of the British register in his mind.

Yet when Captain Parker later mustered his men on that April 19 morning to fight the retreating British on "Battle Road," Jedediah Munroe answered the call and went with his friends into the fire of battle. This time his wounds were fatal—and his admirable courage endures in American history, being one of the few who was wounded by the first shots of the Revolutionary War—and then, on the same morning, returning to fight and to give his life for his country.

Courage of the Old

Many other stories of admirable courage have been told about that morning and afternoon—both in Lexington and Concord and in the fighting during the long British retreat. One event in particular stands out because of the unique individual involved—he was seventy-eight years old! Sam Whittemore lived in Menotomy, present-day Arlington, a small town lying on the path of the late afternoon British retreat to Boston.

Waiting behind the cover of a stone wall, Sam Whittemore fired several shots at the Regulars moving in his direction. The accuracy of this fire quickly drew the attention of many troops, who rushed the wall. One of the attackers was fatally struck by a ball from Whittemore's musket. The Regulars then overwhelmed his lone position and proceeded to shoot him in the head and inflict many other wounds including bayonet stabs, leaving him bleeding profusely and near death. But, by the grace of God and with the help of family and friends, he recovered from his wounds. After the battle he lived to age ninety-eight!

His courage was shown in his willingness, despite his age, to defend his town against overwhelming odds and then, after being left to die, to fight another kind of battle—to overcome his injuries. He was one of many older American men (the oldest, eighty, confronted the Regulars at Concord's Old North Bridge!) who fought, to the consternation and dismay of the British Regulars, with remarkable courage and stubbornness during the battles on that day.

Courage on April 19, 1775—Lessons for Today

The preservation of liberty depends upon the intellectual and moral character of the people

—John Adams

Defense of Justified Values

The essence of the admirable courage displayed on April 19, 1775, was the intent and strength of will to face danger in defense of justified values. This courage was not aggressive or belligerent in its beginnings. Nor was it an unreasonable, obstinate stance or a deliberate assertion of willpower without an underlying moral foundation. It rose far above natural selfish instincts—instead it was the fruit of conscientious planning and careful thought by good people of like mind. Their "facing toward the Regulars" was neither an accident nor an instantaneous one-man show. The militia's overall strategy was pre-planned and well considered—to organize in united defiance to a threat to freedom but not to be the aggressor. This was true of all militia and minutemen in New England.

The moral courage in self-defense at this sunrise set an example for, and became, American military policy for the next two centuries and longer—to act aggressively only in self-defense—and this "defense" must not fire the first shot. This idea clearly includes the principle that, prior to war having actually begun or declared, a strike is justified only if the enemy has already attacked America or its allies. In the present-day nuclear world and consistent with this principle, self-defense is also justified if the enemy's conduct and known intent amount to an imminent and irrevocable violent attack, or if a "line in the sand," a defense-justified ultimatum removing any reasonable doubt of the enemy's intention, has been crossed.

In the case of Lexington, the sudden violent firing of musketry volleys by the British Regulars was not expected and was not foreknown. Importantly, in previous marches by the Regulars into the Massachusetts countryside, other town militia had stood openly against the British but no attack occurred and the Regulars had backed away. This was known by Captain Parker. If he knew for certain that the Regulars would fire when reaching the Common or if the war had already started, then he would have been morally justified in firing first. But he had no such knowledge; the war had not yet started!

The Standard of Admirable Courage

The admirable courage on April 19 is a national standard we ought to follow. Some may disagree with the standard itself—that Captain Parker should have fired first because the British threat was menacing and approaching. But this is different than an existing state of hostilities or an imminent and clear danger of attack against America or its friends. The standard actually used on April 19 is the one that should be used, and has been used in American history, to justify intentional use of arms in defense. This sets us apart from the world.

Some may also assert that the militia should not have fired at all but rather should have willingly submitted to the King's Troops who, after all, represented the existing governing authority. This, it is said, represents the scriptural and ethical standard "to obey the governing authorities." The New Testament is particularly clear on a Christian's duty to obey authorities and to" honor the emperor." Without going too deep into this area of dispute, two things can be said relating to this issue. First, the scriptural admonition of obedience to authorities is directed, of course, to obeying existing and legitimate governmental units, not to someone merely claiming authority. Second, this admonition has limits—authorities are not to be obeyed when they insist on obedience to laws that contradict a Christian's belief or duty.

Self-Defense and Scripture

The teachings of the Bible, considering both the Old Testament and the more intensive revelation of grace and love in the later New Testament, do not advocate or condone aggression, violence, or even hatred toward anyone. To the contrary, the New Testament teaches that, in following and relying on God's grace, Christians should love their enemies and submit to persecution rather than offer physical resistance.

Yet, the Bible does not prohibit justifiable self-defense—there are rare cases in which solely defensive or deterrent actions to immediate threats are recognized as realistic and necessary. Invoking his rights as a Roman citizen, the Apostle Paul threatened his persecutors with the harsh justice of the Roman Empire to prevent their unjustified violence against him. In the Book of Luke, it is recorded that, on the night of his arrest, Jesus told his disciples to buy swords—of course not to perpetrate any aggression or violence but solely as a deterrent against armed attack. Luke 22:36 (Peter later used his sword in an aggressive and attacking manner and was admonished by Jesus for doing so.) In the Roman persecutions during the early centuries of the Christian church, believers at the cost of their lives refused to obey the decrees of Rome.

In the Old Testament, there are examples of resistance to despotic human authority. The Israelites under Moses resisted the Pharaoh of Egypt who had enslaved them. As recorded in the Book of Judges, Gideon and his 300 men fought against the ruling Midianites and Samson against the ruling Philistines.

It is not the purpose here to reach a conclusion, in light of religious teachings or current ethical values, concerning the moral justification for the American Revolution itself. It is noteworthy, however, that most Puritan ministers in New England in 1775, who were Bible–believing and were experiencing the turmoil of that time and the harsh British oppression, as well as many church ministers throughout the colonies, were patriots who supported resistance to the British attacks.

As for individual Christian behavior toward others, the New Testament standard is to refrain from violence and intentional injury, especially taken in revenge. "If it be possible, as much as lieth in you, live peaceably with all men." (Romans 12:18) For personal ethics, this standard might be considered higher than the bar of morality set at Lexington. In any case, it is without doubt consistent with an appeal to Americans to not intentionally injure others except in moral self-defense.

It should be observed that this scriptural teaching of living at peace with others, given by the Apostle Paul, who passed on a high and morally perfect ideal, nevertheless recognizes that peace may not be possible if the attacking person, nation, or group, rather than yourself, is in control of the situation and compels the violence that cannot be prevented. This seems to fit what happened at Lexington.

The "Governing Authorities" in 1775

In April 1775, insofar as almost all people in Massachusetts were concerned, the primary and legitimate governmental units in New England were the elected Provincial Congress (although considered treasonous by the British), local town assemblies and town meetings, and locally elected officials. This was basically true in the other colonies as well, although some areas of the country had larger numbers of Tories, or Loyalists, than other places.

By early 1775, England, by reason of its many oppressive actions, not the least of which was its revocation of the self-government clauses of the colonial charters and setting up military rule, had for all practical purposes forfeited its authority and respect. The only exception was, up to a limit, continuing colonial loyalty to and respect for King George III himself. Obedience to locally elected leadership and self-governing bodies was paramount and even went beyond opposing royal decrees. Notably, according to historical accounts, in the town of Lexington in April 1775, this reality of life was reflected in the fact that not one British Loyalist could be found in the entire population of 750.

Admirable Courage and Interpersonal Actions

A wise and frugal government...shall restrain men from injuring one another.

—Thomas Jefferson

In addition to the application of admirable courage in the area of military policy or with respect to governmental authority, logically this virtue has relevance today to individual actions—that is, interpersonal behavior. This applies to how we should:

- Relate in a physical way to our fellow citizens
- Behave in a society when there is aggression or tendencies toward violence
- Drive our vehicles amid threats of road rage
- Live within our families when bitter disagreements arise
- Engage in business or work where aggression is sometimes just below the surface
- Settle our disputes and respond to insults
- Conduct ourselves in athletic competition both as participants and spectators.

In short, how should each of us personally live in physical relation to others? Using the admirable courage exemplified by the minutemen on April 19, 1775 as a standard, the answer to this question is this: Physical violence or intentional injury inflicted on others is only justified when exercised in the act of defending or protecting against physical harm or against actions intended to cause physical harm that are unquestionably and imminently threatened, where there also exists a moral foundation for the defensive action. This could be called admirable self-defense.

Let's look at some examples. If an armed criminal robs a store and is confronted by an armed cashier, it would *not* be admirable (or legal) self-defense for the robber to shoot the cashier "in self defense." The same goes for a criminal shooting at pursuing police, a child retaliating when being punished by a parent, a husband or wife physically abusing an insulting spouse, a driver using violent road rage after being cut off or subjected to insults on the highway, or an athlete intentionally injuring an opponent in any athletic competition. None of these actions of physical retaliation or intentional physical injury are morally justified.

Intentional Violence in Athletics and Entertainment

Being even more specific, let's look at some athletic events popular today. Cage fighting (or "ultimate fighting") or even boxing without protective gear, professional wrestling, and modern, physical contact sports such as football and hockey, *under current rules*, involve without any question intentional infliction of injury without a moral foundation (irrespective of the mutual consent of the participants). The same is true of videos and films that condone, by willingly portraying and glorifying, unrestrained and intentional violence with no moral justification. These activities clearly violate the virtue of admirable self-defense held by our founding patriots.

But even beyond this, the unjustified and unnecessary (and well-documented) individual injuries that are part and parcel of now socially accepted intentionally violent athletic contests, when considered together, cause serious damage to the overall physical strength, moral fiber, and well-being of the nation. These consequences are in addition to the great cost in medical treatment for intentionally caused injuries, the personal devastation of families and careers, and the heartbreaking impact on enjoyment of life and the ability to work and be a productive citizen long after any athletic glory has faded away. Is a serious head, neck, or leg injury, or any injury to a young man or woman, intentionally inflicted or intentionally permitted without moral justification, worth the cost—or worth the brief seconds of glory and thrill or the excitement of the applauding, screaming crowds that filled the atmosphere for a moment in time?

How do these injuries in violent athletics, some fatal and many disabling young people for life, fulfill the "pursuit of happiness"? How do they promote the "general welfare"? How can they be squared with the principle of moral self-defense? How are they possibly consistent with any peaceful religion? It is not to be understood that this is an argument for a governmental ban on intentionally violent sports—but rather it is an appeal for all Americans to (1) clearly recognize, when so apparent, violations of our fundamental, historic, and religious values, and (2) resolutely and voluntarily work to change the "sword" of morally unjustified violence into "ploughshares" of wholesome, uplifting, and virtuous human interactivity. This is possible to do.

Chapter Six

Purposeful Moral Unity

Unity in 1775

It is not in numbers, but in unity, that our great strength lies.

—Thomas Paine

The virtue of unity in 1775 was a tangible and active force in the revolutionary break with England. This can be called purposeful moral unity—because it was directed at achieving a common, overarching, worthy goal, namely freedom from autocratic governmental oppression.

By contrast, in our time the "virtue" of accepting various cultural values or actions regardless of moral merit, in the name of "diversity" and not unity, is advocated and praised, almost venerated, by leading universities and news outlets beyond what anyone would recognize as sensible in 1775. This includes the acceptance or "affirmation" of different and often conflicting values, even those in many instances separated by light years on the infinite continuum of conceivable "values." Examples of this include affirmation of cultures in which: women and sometimes even children are essentially treated as property; political and economic corruption and bribery are the rule; Christianity is barred but other religions of intolerance are permitted or even promoted; laboring people are routinely abused; democracy is suppressed or twisted to allow despotic rule; and even where indolence and idleness are considered equivalent or even superior values to industriousness and punctuality. This is not to suggest we should look down on or injure these cultures. Far from it. But if at all possible these practices should not, in the name of diversity or "moral equivalency," be praised or financially assisted (excepting only aid to a country in case of a natural disaster). The purposeful moral unity of the minutemen is better and stronger than following contradictory diversity.

Women and Men Unified for the Cause of Liberty

In 1775 when, it is true, women's rights, especially political rights, in America and throughout the world were very restricted, the kind of repression of the female sex witnessed today in certain areas of the world would nonetheless have been totally rejected in America. In practice, American women in that time were very much an active and open part of society—and had much to say in the business of the home and in the relationships of life. They were neither kept hidden from sight, nor suppressed, nor isolated from social activity. In the battle of Lexington, as will be seen shortly, they played an extremely important role in the ultimately successful American opposition to the attack by the British Regulars, both at Lexington and Concord and during the rest of the War.

The wives of American militiamen and minutemen did not sit idly at home. Several examples of important contributions of women on April 19, 1775, are to be noted. While the men were in the field, women kept busy making bullets or "cartridges" (gunpowder casings for muskets), preparing food for the men, caring for and protecting frightened children, and blockading windows and doors of their homes in case the Regulars attempted to break in (not an unrealistic possibility).

In one town on that April 19, while the men were gone, the wives formed their own company of militia—and used this force to go on armed patrols near their homes. In the process they captured a Tory spy who was turned over to patriot authorities. Rebecca Barrett, the wife of Colonel

Barrett, minutemen leader at Concord, was ordered by British officers to give them breakfast when they invaded her home looking for military "stores." She consented to their demand—quoting, to the dismay of the officers, the Biblical admonition she should "feed our enemies." She refused their offer of compensation—but was forced to accept the coins when they threw the money at her. Other women in Concord deceived marauding British soldiers searching homes and farms. In essence, the colonial women bravely told, or hinted to, the British soldiers that rooms with closed or locked doors were occupied by "indisposed ladies" when in fact the rooms contained military provisions. The British, although now at war, scrupulously observed these pleas for feminine privacy—and consequently the military supplies were untouched.

In summary, the women of this time were unified, in heart and effective action, with the men in opposition to the attack on their freedom by the British Regulars.

African American Unity with the Patriots

The same is true of African Americans. Although most were slaves or servants during that period, yet in their social and working relationships, in New England in particular, many were very much involved and supportive of the patriot side in the Revolution and also were astute observers of British oppression. They were united with other patriots against the British view of the world—that of arbitrary rule by the powerful and aggressive military suppression of any dissent or resistance. In their patriotic stand, it would seem that, in the colonists' fight for freedom and self-government, African Americans foresaw and aspired to the future vision of their own freedom that would come ninety years later.

Prince Estabrook

The prime example of African American oneness with the patriot cause was Prince Estabrook, the slave who was a member of the militia at Lexington and was wounded at the April 19 sunrise. As we have noted, this was not his only contribution in the War. He went on to serve with distinction in other campaigns and eventually won his own freedom. He was not the only one. Many other slaves and freed ex-slaves fought on the American side. The British officer who brandished his sword just before the Regulars' charge at the Lexington Common, Major Pitcairn, was killed in the Battle of Bunker Hill two months later. Historians record that the fatal shot was fired by a freed ex-slave on the American side. (It is an interesting and ironic fact of history that Major Pitcairn was buried in a crypt under the Old North Church, the very place that was the source of the warning to Americans of the attack led by him at Lexington.)

A Brave African American Woman

Special insight into the sympathies of African Americans in 1775 is found in a pre-battle story of a black woman servant at a countryside inn in Massachusetts in February of that year. She was serving food to poorly disguised British officers who had stopped at a small inn to take a dinner break during their mission of espionage. They were out checking the terrain and investigating the best military routes to the town of Worcester, which was a possible military target of the British before they had decided on Concord.

The alert servant woman immediately recognized the men were British spies. Responding to their suspicious compliments about the local countryside, she told them point blank, "and we have fine fellows to defend it!" She then let them know in unmistakable terms she knew their purpose. Knowing their mission had been discovered, the frightened officers quickly got up and left. Thereafter they were closely observed by other patriots until they returned to Boston.

It can be seen from this alert and observant woman's brief but courageous conversation with the officers ("we have fine fellows to defend it") that she identified with the minutemen and the militia who were defending the colonists' freedom. This was not the only occasion she had confronted British spies. She had an uncanny ability of recognizing who they were and letting them know they were headed for trouble. She was a patriot, standing up for a cause she knew to be right.

Unity of the Minutemen

Perhaps the greatest display of unity that sunrise was shown by the militia who responded to Captain Parker's first call to come to the Common. This force, 146 men and teenage boys, comprised about 18 percent of the town's population. Other Massachusetts towns had similar percentages of minutemen and militia. In 2012, if the same percentage of the U.S. population entered military service as did the militia in 1775, we would have almost 55 million male volunteers, not to mention the millions of women who would also be willing to serve. And it should not be forgotten that, in 1775, the Lexington men responded again later in the morning to a second muster and returned to the battle. Many went on to serve in later Revolutionary War campaigns including the Battle of Bunker Hill in June 1775. The minutemen each were different in many ways, of course, but all had a clear and persistent oneness of purpose—to serve the cause of freedom.

Purposeful Moral Unity on April 19, 1775— Lessons For Today

Unity to Achieve a Common and Worthy Goal

Unity for a purpose, a moral purpose, was evident in the actions of American women at the time of Lexington. They supported the cause of freedom with the same energy and diligence as did the men. But this did not mean women had the same role. Nor does it mean that the failure of women to be in the militia or the term "minutemen" itself was a violation of human rights. There is no violation of the virtue of unity if different duties are given to or assumed by different groups however separated. The value of unity is not simply to have oneness. The overriding attribute is to achieve a common worthy goal—and this not only allows different roles but requires them to reach the goal.

In 1775 there was no complaint by women that they were denied the opportunity to serve. They did serve—but in that time in a special and necessary way—protecting home and children, supplying the needs of those in the field, and, maybe most needed, praying for success and the safety of the men in battle.

April 19, 1775, also tells us that unity for a moral purpose transcends age, race, and background. The militia included all capable men and teenagers—and even a black slave who fought with them. The men over fifty did not complain they were on the "alarm list" and not designated as militia or minutemen. Prince Estabrook as far as we know did not complain about his status. He was willing to serve. The black servant woman who recognized the British spies said "we" have fine men to defend our country. She did not rise up and demand her rights nor did she rush to join the British—she was defending American rights, knowing somehow, someway, the tide of history was on the side of freedom including her own.

This is not to say an individual should not defend his or her rights. There is a time for that but also a time for unifying behind a common moral purpose greater in value than each individual. It is important to add that the egnigmatic facts that Americans fought for freedom against the British while at the same time allowing slavery were recognized in 1775 as contradictory, that is, something wasn't right. Because of the realization of this contradiction, it is fair to say that there was a general and growing consciousness, especially in New England, that in a country where liberty is a sacred right, slavery could not last forever and that, in time, the slaves would and must be free. This feeling probably was most strong among the slaves themselves of course but the ultimate fate of slavery, its end, was also envisioned and desired by leading patriots themselves including John Adams, George Washington, Sam Adams, Patrick Henry, James Madison, and Thomas Jefferson.

The exclusion of women from active political participation was also recognized as something that needed to be changed. Abigail Adams, wife of John Adams our second President, was especially outspoken about women's rights and the necessity of women having a say in governmental decisions. In time, after more than a century, this injustice too was rectified.

Today's Need for Purposeful Moral Unity

The fact that almost all able men and boys answered the call at that sunrise shows us that unity is most effective when there is universal participation in a worthy purpose. Why can't we have that today? Why do so few answer the call to serve our country? Why do so few volunteer for important work in civic groups, charities, and religious groups? Why do some finally join a group—but only to receive a special reward, recognition, or compensation?

The same kind of oneness of purpose shown in 1775 is needed in our time in order to:

- Protect freedom from arbitrary and overreaching government actions
- Clearly define worthy goals and pursue them to a successful result
- Make sure our laws, regulations, and court rulings do not snuff out the spark of human initiative or prevent worthwhile endeavors
- Work together to solve and stop assaults on our physical well-being through wiser retention, punishment, and restriction of violent criminals— the protection of women from violent men and children from abuse is a very strong, often ignored, need today

- Provide through churches and charities and other groups the necessary generosity to help those who cannot help themselves, and

- Join together in locally organized groups to support and pay for high-quality and nonviolent education for our youth without excessive government money or unreasonable or ungodly direction and control.

Chapter Seven

Virtuous Reliability

Examples of Reliability in 1775

To say what may be self-evident, personal reliability is undoubtedly a major shortcoming in our lives today. In 1775, this virtue of course was not common to everyone. But there are so many examples of it in the context of the Battle of Lexington that it must have been the rule and not the exception in that time and place. Again, the reliability at that time, which should be respected and honored, was practiced for a worthy and virtuous cause. Many Loyalists were paid spies for the British, and very reliable in their service to the British, but this was not virtuous reliability. Let's look then at real examples of virtuous reliability.

Sam Adams

No man in Congress, if any, equaled Sam Adams; and none did more than he, to originate and sustain revolutionary measures in Congress.

I can truly say he was a great man.

I always considered him as more important than any other member, the fountain of our important measures.

—Thomas Jefferson on Sam Adams

The American Revolution and its ultimate success was the combined product of many patriots. This hall of fame would include George Washington, Thomas Jefferson, Patrick Henry, John Adams, Paul Revere, James Otis, Sam Adams, John Hancock, Thomas Paine, Ben Franklin, James Madison, Alexander Hamilton, Henry Knox, Nathaniel Greene, Ethan Allen, Daniel Morgan, John Paul Jones, and so many others—including, of course, the members of the Continental Congress and all of the volunteers who served in militias and with the Continental Army and American Navy, and wives and families.

Sam Adams—Leader of the Revolution, Patriarch of Liberty, and a Founding Father

But if one had to name a single individual who was most responsible for motivating or causing the American Revolution and its accomplishment of achieving liberty and preserving self-government, that person would be Sam Adams of Boston. From the Stamp Act in 1765, to the Boston Tea Party in 1773, to the Battle at Lexington, to the Declaration of Independence in 1776, Sam Adams was in the very center, at the heart, of America's struggle toward liberty and independence.

Adams was a powerful and inspiring writer, leader, and organizer, and the people in Massachusetts somehow grasped that his ideas and goals were worthy and right. And they followed him—in many elections he was elected, often by over a 95 percent vote, to the Colonial Massachusetts House of Representatives and to the Continental Congress. A cousin of the future President and fellow revolutionary, John Adams, Sam Adams was an early and often lone visionary of America's destiny of liberty. He could almost see into the future—and was intent on making that future happen!

Sam Adams, Leader of the American Revolution

Not only was he a great leader in the pursuit of freedom, Sam Adams was reliable. A modest and humble man, not the greatest orator and not a military hero, he had no regard for his own comforts or desires, only for America and the cause of freedom. Although highly educated, earning a Masters Degree from Harvard at twenty-one, he was a man who knew poverty and hard times. He even wore donated clothes to attend the Continental Congress to which he was elected by the people of Massachusetts. The British, including the King of England and General Gage in Boston, were fully aware of Sam Adams' great influence with the populace and desperately wanted him out of the way. As a result, even before the Battle of Lexington, Adams was targeted along with John Hancock for arrest and deportation to England to face trial for treason, with hanging the likely result.

A Futile Attempt at Bribery

General Gage had met with success in bribing some Americans to be spies for the British. These spies pretended to be American patriots but in fact were paid Loyalists. One of the spies in Massachusetts appears to have been Dr. Benjamin Church, a close patriot associate of both Adams and Hancock and also of Paul Revere. (Although insisting on his innocence, Church's actions were later discovered and he was banished from America. He was lost at sea.)

Having met success with Dr. Church, Gage decided he would try to lure Sam Adams to the British camp or at least to neutrality. So in the summer of 1774, General Gage, through a personal military agent, made a tantalizing offer to Adams—if Adams stopped his resistance activities and retired from the scene (became "a peaceable subject'), Gage would insure that Adams would receive a substantial annual cash payment for life. And further, the representative from General Gage made the point, which Gage probably hoped would appeal to Adams' sense of duty, that Adams would receive the very valuable intangible benefit of knowing he had "made peace with his King." Without hesitation, Sam

Adams rejected the bribe—advising Gage's messenger that no amount of money would cause him to betray the righteous cause of his country. As for peace with the King, Adams, looking directly at the messenger, replied with conviction and a steady voice that long ago he had made his peace with the "King of Kings."

Here again was reliability to be admired and encouraged. Sam Adams was a poor man, but no earthly gain and no earthly peace could persuade him to give up the cause of America. And he took his stand at the risk of his life. For in June 1775, after the Battle of Lexington, General Gage made *two* exceptions to an offer of a general pardon to everyone who would renounce the patriots' cause and return to British allegiance—those two exceptions, those who could *never* receive a pardon, were Sam Adams and John Hancock!

God forgive them for they know not what they do.

—Thomas Jefferson upon hearing that people were critical
of Sam Adams many years after the Revolution

Sam Adams in History

Yet, Sam Adams does not have a good reputation among historians. He has been called an incendiary firebrand, a rabble rouser, a mob leader, and a radical instigator of violence and mayhem. These accusations are undeserved. Although his writings and speeches inspired passionate feelings and revolutionary fervor, there seems to be little direct evidence he instigated wanton violence except perhaps for the Boston Tea Party which he is credited with organizing. But importantly, the Boston Tea Party, although destroying 342 chests of tea by dumping them into Boston Harbor, caused no destruction of any other property and no injury to any person.

Sam Adams was one of the few patriot leaders who, very early in the resistance to the British and several years before the Battle of Lexington, understood England's real intention—to use their overwhelming military superiority, once and for all, to suppress any aspirations of freedom and ideas of self-government in America. Other American patriots who clearly saw this reality in those early years were Patrick Henry and, immediately after the Battle of Lexington, Thomas Jefferson, John Adams, George Washington, and Thomas Paine.

Thomas Jefferson, author of the Declaration of Independence. He was one of the few who understood the true intentions of the British in 1775. He recognized Sam Adams as the father of the American Revolution.

Before the War started, King George III and a large majority in the English Parliament considered the Americans to be disloyal subjects who needed to be taught a severe lesson in obedience and submission—to be compelled by overwhelming brute force and, if necessary, bloodshed, to obey the will of Parliament and the King's decrees without question. Not only did Sam Adams understand these British intentions, he, along with Patrick Henry and Thomas Jefferson, were totally confident that America, despite the massive, unparalleled military and economic power of the British Empire, would succeed in their resistance to the coming assault.

Probably the best example of Adams' confidence and vision was displayed in his historic speech to the Continental Congress during the bleakest days of the War, September 1777, when all seemed lost. He closed with these words:

"Let us rely in humble confidence on Him who is mighty to save. Good tidings will soon arrive. We shall never be abandoned by Heaven while we act worthy of its aid and protection."

Just a month later came the news of the great American victory at Saratoga, New York, the decisive turning point in the War!

John Hancock

We fear not death.

—John Hancock, 1774

Before considering the reliability of Paul Revere, a few words are appropriate concerning Sam Adams' friend and co-patriot, John Hancock. Like Adams, Hancock was a graduate of Harvard. Other than that, the two men were very different in age, background, and temperament. Hancock, thirty-eight in 1775, was wealthy, having inherited a large fortune from his uncle including a successful shipping business. He enjoyed expensive clothes and fine dining. He owned costly articles of personal property and was meticulous in his dress and personal habits. Unlike Adams, he was not a deep visionary thinker. Also unlike Adams, John Hancock was extremely capable at business matters. He did not have Adams' talent for writing and organizing.

Historians relate that Hancock was somewhat vain and pretentious—quite concerned about what others thought of him. In contrast, Sam Adams, age fifty-two in April 1775, his mind and life fixed on making the Revolution happen, was totally unconcerned about what others thought of him. Yet Hancock, handsome, sociable, and engaging, was extremely popular with the people (he was elected the first governor of Massachusetts after the Revolution), probably more popular than Adams—and as a result he was an immense advantage and help to Sam Adams in organizing revolutionary efforts.

Hancock consistently shared his wealth to support the revolutionary cause and also to help those in need. He was courageous—as he, a wealthy merchant, stood to lose more in terms of property than almost anyone else in America if the revolution was not successful. And the chances for its success often looked dim. Yet he always bravely stood his ground in defiance of the British. "Pledging our fortunes" had real meaning for John Hancock when he signed the Declaration of Independence.

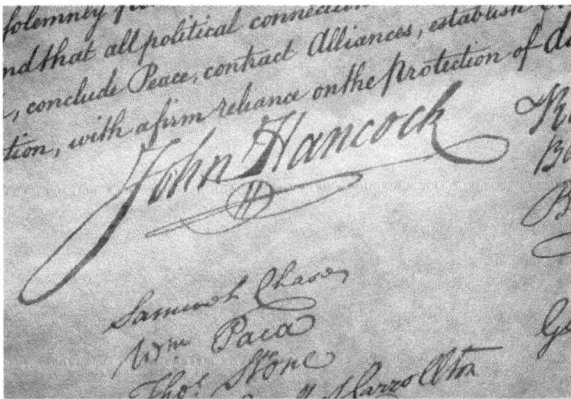

John Hancock's famous signature on the Declaration of Independence. Fearless in his opposition to the British, John Hancock was in Lexington with Sam Adams on the morning of April 19, 1775, when the American Revolutionary War started.

He also was a very capable politician and administrator. This was recognized by his fellow patriots. He was elected to both the office of president of the Massachusetts Provincial Congress and president of the Second Continental Congress (the representative body of all American colonies) that met in Philadelphia soon after the battle of Lexington. He served several years as Treasurer of Harvard University. And as we have previously seen, he was elected the first post-war governor of Masschusetts. John Hancock was also President of the Massachusetts Convention that approved the U.S Constitution many years after the Revolution. When as a representative from Massachusetts and as President of the Continental Congress, he signed the Declaration of Independence with his famous signature, he is said to have remarked he wanted King George III (known for poor vision) to see his signature without having to use spectacles.

His reputation for courage and reliability has lived on. Almost two centuries later, an aircraft carrier that served with great distinction in World War II and Korea was named after him, as are many businesses and famous buildings in America today.

John Hancock Tower, Boston

John Hancock Center, Chicago

Paul Revere

If there is an epitome of reliability (and courage!) in American history, it would be Paul Revere. In addition to his famous Midnight Ride on April 18-19, 1775, he made at least sixteen other trips for the patriots' cause. Those times, of course, preceded the telegraph and other modern communication methods—and urgent messages and important news had to be delivered on horseback by dependable couriers. Many of Paul Revere's rides delivered news between Boston, where revolutionary activity was high, and Philadelphia, where the Continental Congress was meeting, a journey of 300 miles. Neither blistering heat nor blinding snow storms nor sheets of cold rain deterred him. At least three long rides were made in the dead of winter. There is no record of him turning back or giving up. He did all this while supporting 16 children (each of his two wives had eight children—he married the second after the first died) and actively serving in many civic and patriot groups.

Not only are his many rides proof of his exceptional reliability, his actions on the night of April 19, 1775, show his true intentions, that is, the reason why he made his rides. It was *not* to gain glory or profit for himself—to be admired or rewarded as the one who delivered the message. Paul Revere's only intent was to get the message through—and to do this he made sure the message was delivered even if he could not do it. Having his rowboat ready on the banks of the Charles River and arranging for the lantern signals in the Old North Church show the depth of his reliability—doing everything he could, in terms of planning, anticipating problems, and thinking things through, to guarantee the message in the cause of freedom was delivered. The essence of his reliability, then, was not doing important tasks by himself but rather carefully and conscientiously ensuring the mission or job was accomplished.

The Minutemen

We need no persuasion that the minutemen and militia of New England were reliable. Yet two important and inspiring facts should be emphasized. First, the militia and minutemen came from all parts of society and were of all ages (except for officially designated minutemen who were all young men). Counting the alarm lists, the militia in fact consisted of all physically able men and all boys sixteen and over. And they showed up. In other words, almost all men and boys were dependable!

Secondly, consider the time of day the Lexington militia was called out—it was first at 1:00 a.m. and then at 4:30 a.m.! At the hour when sleep was their strong desire (especially for teenagers and older men!), all were willing to get up and leave their homes and warm beds, not only to muster on the Lexington Common but to knowingly face death for the cause of liberty. This reliability has to challenge everyone today.

Virtuous Reliability on April 19, 1775— Lessons for Today

We learn this meaning of virtuous reliability from the patriots' examples of that time—it is an inner conviction or obligation placed into continuous action to achieve a worthy or virtuous goal. In the example of Sam Adams, this was shown by his constant and faithful leadership in the worthy fight for freedom. It was constant because he was in the forefront of the Revolution from beginning to end—and, as many others, he continued to serve his country and his state after the War to ensure its success was not wasted. It was faithful because he rejected any temptation to give up. He refused to accept any reward, no matter how great or attractive, to forsake his "righteous duty" as he saw it.

In the case of Paul Revere, we see the importance of conscientious preparation and an unselfish attitude to leave nothing undone to accomplish a goal. With the minutemen, reliability is shown in their almost universal willingness to "be there" and "do it" regardless of the hour or sacrifice that was necessary and despite the dangers that were waiting.

We must do the same! Whatever our calling or duty, if it is worthy and right and of benefit to others, we need to:

- Be faithful to our duty and not be thrown off track, not dissuaded, by distracting temptations or appeals to our own personal comfort or selfish desires.

- Persist toward worthy goals and overcome, with the essential aid of God and help of others, all difficulties and seemingly insurmountable obstacles that are in the way.

- Keep commitments ("do what you're supposed to do, when you are supposed to do it and without someone telling you to do it"), "be there," and not use excuses to avoid keeping promises. And always be willing to ask for advice and help.

- Be willing to face and overcome personal inconveniences (such as early hours and bad weather) and fears of danger to meet a worthy commitment.

- Be optimistic and trusting, confident the goal will be achieved even though days and hours may be dark with discouragement or danger.

Chapter Eight

The Desire for Secure Peace

When reading about the American Revolution, one might get the impression that early Americans were not peaceful—rather that they were warlike and aggressive in their resistance to British rule. This is not the case. Because of many internecine struggles with native populations and with the French, especially the recent French and Indian War, Americans in the late 1700s understood the horror and tragedy of war. People came to America looking for a new life—including getting away from the perpetual conflicts in Europe—certainly not seeking war, death, or suffering. So the vast majority were peaceful and law-abiding. As we have previously seen, John Greenleaf Whittier in his poem "Lexington" wrote this about the Lexington militia: "Their feet had trodden peaceful ways—no battle joy was theirs—they loved not strife, they dreaded pain."

A Unique and Inspirational Perspective on Peace

a time of war, and a time of peace

--Ecclesiastes 3:8b

The early patriots had a unique and inspirational perspective on "peace." Peace was often mentioned in the same breath with words like "harmony," "tranquility," "felicity," "happiness," "prosperity," "national morality," and the "absence of evils."

The United States Constitution refers to the "blessings of liberty." Peace, then, was the result of an effort to earn it by justified efforts and then to cultivate it through forgiveness and reconciliation. (It is interesting and important to note that this ingrained American attitude of winning and then forgiving was evident in America's treatment of Germany and Japan after World War II) Peace was not simply the absence of war—instead it was the end of war. It was the security of freedom, the fruit of victory in a struggle against despotism.

In his "Liberty or Death Speech" given at St. John's Church in Richmond, Virginia, shortly before the Battle of Lexington, Patrick Henry declared "Gentlemen may cry peace, peace, but there is no peace"—then crying out "Is life so dear or peace so sweet as to be purchased at the price of chains or slavery? Forbid it Almighty God!" The colonists did not want war, but dreaded the alternative more. Going the extra mile to avoid war, they sent many petitions to Parliament and the King of England, offering compromise and negotiation—then waited patiently for any positive hint or willingness to work out the differences between the two sides. All petitions were rejected or ignored—and instead were met by increased military threats that had unmistakable intent.

Winning a Secure Peace

Our plan is peace forever.

—Thomas Paine

The Declaration of Independence is best known for its proclamation that "all men are created equal." Yet, most of the Declaration is a detailed recital of twenty-seven carefully explained reasons why America had no choice but to fight for its freedom. According to the Declaration, the choice for Americans was either fight or submit to "absolute despotism" and "absolute tyranny." Thomas Jefferson and Patrick

Henry, in 1776, had become of the same mind—peace, secure peace, had to be fought for and won.

This desire for secure peace in 1775, therefore, was a longing for harmony, reconciliation ("in peace, Friends!"), happiness, and freedom. The Lexington minutemen were not aggressors; rather they wanted and sought a secure peace—the peace of enjoying freedom—that was earned by standing against, at the cost of sacrificing their own lives, those who wanted the "peace" of brute force.

The Desire for Secure Peace on April 19, 1775—Lessons for Today

Secure Peace Must be Earned.

Considering the values of the Lexington Minutemen and founding American patriots, what comes first to mind about secure peace on earth is that it must be earned. This kind of peace in families, in neighborhoods, in churches, between political parties, between individuals, and among nations requires a great and continuous *mutual effort*. "My way or the highway" is certainly not a path to secure peace.

Secure Peace Through Meetings.

One way to achieve and maintain secure peace is simply to have meetings, many of them, as did the people of Lexington, the congregation of the Lexington church, and all the people in early America for that matter. This history plus common sense tell us that the more people meet the better off we are. That the churches of the New England minutemen were called "meetinghouses" is proof of their strong confidence in meetings. They knew that many heads are better than one—it is quite astonishing how better ideas, better conclusions, and better results almost magically spring out of the conversations and give-and-take of meetings. Even a brilliant idea offered by one person is almost always improved in some way at a meeting.

And group-developed ideas are not the only goal of a meeting—equally important are the implementation process and timing for making the jointly approved idea actually work. This requires group input. The final objective is not compromise but the overall best practical result, owned by everyone, created by an exchange of thinking. In making decisions as a group, early Americans accomplished this by making resolution of disagreements a reality through the acceptance of a majority vote after input from all present. This culture of localized meetings, which seems to be at the very heart of self-government and democracy, was in direct opposition to the atmosphere of royal fiat and centralized rule emanating from England.

Of course, there are scorpions, rattlesnakes, raging bulls, and absentees in this world. No amount of meetings or exchanges of ideas will work when an opponent is not acting in good faith or will not meet at all. A simple, modern-day illustration of the importance of being an active participant in meetings is the grading structure created by a kindergarten teacher. To receive a good grade, the children not only have to sit in a circle but also *participate* in the circle in a positive, not dominating, way. All have to share and listen. Just being present is not good enough to achieve peace. In 1775, the colonists sought meetings and give-and-take participation with the British, but to no avail. Unfortunately, submission was the only offer America received.

Working and Standing Up for Secure Peace

If meetings fail to achieve peace, early American patriots showed us other avenues. Of real importance is working and standing for peace—taking action and steps that will lead to peace. At Lexington, the action taken was standing on the Common and physically defying unjustified force. A bully will often back down if one stands up to him.

Although not successful in preventing the attack at Lexington, this way of achieving peace did ultimately succeed—when America and the British signed their peace treaty in Paris in 1783.

Secure Peace Through Unity

A third avenue to secure peace taught by the minutemen is acting in unity. The Lexington militia was not only unified, but all towns in New England were likewise unified in their opposition to the British threat despite the ongoing risk of being arrested by British authorities and the existence (and danger) of a small minority of Loyalists to the Crown.. When the alarm sounded and British Regulars attacked, the minutemen of all towns for miles around came to help—and it was their common effort that drove the British back to their barracks in Boston. This was really a miniature version of the resistance during the Revolutionary War by the united colonies, who banded together, despite separation by great distances and differences in culture between North and South and the Middle Colonies, to declare independence and fight together, under George Washington, for the peace that eventually was won.

Gaining Allies for Secure Peace

A fourth way of achieving peace, also used in the Revolutionary War, is to gain allies to stand with you. Using the schoolyard analogy, a bully is likely to back down not only when "stood up to" but, even more so, when friends stand united against him. This is exactly what happened when France joined the battle against the British following the American victory at Saratoga, New York, in October 1777. The War could not have been won without the French.

Not only did America gain allies, the founding patriots believed without wavering that they would get them well before it even happened. In his historic speech at St. John's

Church on April 23, 1775, Patrick Henry, looking confidently into the future, spoke these visionary words:

> "Besides, sir, we shall not fight our battles alone. There is a just God who presides over the destinies of nations and who will raise up friends to fight our battles for us."

Patience and Gaining Secure Peace.

An indispensable resource for secure peace, shown to us by early Americans, is patience. In the worst times of the War— the defeats at Brooklyn and at Fort Lee on the Manhattan heights overlooking the Hudson River in New York; Washington's retreat across New Jersey; the British occupation of Philadelphia; the harsh cold, hunger, and despair of Valley Forge; and defeats in many battles—the patriot founders never lost hope and never gave up. Patient persistence, with diligent prayer, can win a secure peace.

Kindness and Gaining Secure Peace.

Incredibly, there appear to have been many instances of kindness and caring on April 19, 1775. Although the fighting that day was bitter, the people of Eastern Massachusetts, particularly physicians, cared for the captured wounded British Regulars, undoubtedly with the same compassion that was shown to injured minutemen. Some of the captured Regulars were even permitted to stay and make their home in Massachusetts. And when the British officers demanded food and breakfast from patriot women, it was not denied them, even though the British were "the enemy."

These examples have important implications for both interpersonal and international peace today. The fire in the heart of your enemy can be dampened with a kind deed or even a kind word. "A soft answer turneth away wrath." (Psalm 15:1a.) Concerning peace with other countries and cultures, it would seem that natural and man-caused disasters, happening almost every day, offer an opportunity to achieve peace by helping enemy and potential enemy nations. As just one example, if an earthquake were to strike Iran, America should be the first to offer help. In fact, the United States should have a reserve set aside for precisely these kinds of events. The motivation should be strictly unselfish—a dividend of peace will be reaped without even thinking about it. The same mindset should prevail even in the absence of a natural disaster. For example, using this reserve, the United States could offer help to our enemies to prevent injuries and death in the event of a likely calamity. The old proverb "You can catch more flies with honey than vinegar" applies to both personal and world peace! Of course, there should be no effort to control any nation, and interference in a nation's internal affairs should be carefully avoided. This "peace reserve" should never be systematized as "foreign aid" lest its purpose be corrupted.

Chapter Nine

Noble Freedom

We are a nation that has a government—not the other way around. And this makes us special among the nations of the earth. Our government has no power except that granted it by the people.

—Ronald Reagan

Freedom From Arbitrary Power

The words "freedom" and "liberty" have many meanings, often contradictory or misunderstood. One popular meaning is being free of rules. Another is the right to act without physical restraint or to be free of restraints such as release from prison. A third is to do what you want regardless of any existing boundaries that apply to you.

These are not the meanings given to freedom by the minutemen and by the American founders in 1775. The freedom they wanted and defended was freedom from arbitrary, or far-away, nonrepresentative, centralized power. It was *not* freedom to do as they pleased that was desired. The meetinghouse where the minutemen met and made decisions, the militia company they joined that had written bylaws, and the religious obligations they honored, convincingly prove they did not oppose rules. To them, it was only common sense that rules and laws were necessary. But they had to be those that the local majority or their direct representatives made or accepted or that an individual voluntarily accepted. For example, an individual voluntarily committed to the Puritan "Covenant" (explained in chapter 10). When joining the militia, the members voluntarily made a covenant to abide by the rules of the militia association. The minutemen were also obligated to the ordinances passed by majority vote in their town and by the laws passed by the Massachusetts Provincial Congress. These were serious restraints on their liberty. But they were representative, voted-upon restraints.

In his day, Patrick Henry was probably the most respected and successful lawyer in Virginia. He knew and followed the "Common Law," or prior case law, which came from English and American legal precedent. The Common Law served as a check on the power of judges—in the cases before them they had to follow past settled court decisions in similar cases and not simply do as they pleased. The Common Law, tested over time, governed the everyday affairs of people. (In large measure, it still does this today.). Therefore, when Patrick Henry called out for "liberty or death," he by no means was demanding a license to do anything free of laws. He was exalting liberty from despotic, nonrepresentative, or arbitrary centralized control and nothing more.

Moreover, the colonies did not join together to declare independence in order to live in anarchy—they knew all too well that humans (and their governments) needed restrictions. But the restrictions had to be self-determined by majority vote, which is why of course the Constitution was written. The Constitution itself is proof that the founders of America wanted governmental laws and restraints on human behavior based on self-determination and majority vote.

For the minutemen, freedom also implied its proper and gainful use. They of course believed in freedom of opportunity (though not yet, in that historical period, extended to women and slaves) but were equally committed to actually *using* that opportunity. The freedom they sought included and required hard work for its fulfillment. They were in fact hard-working farmers and tradesmen. Freedom to them also included active participation in their church and in the community. In the same way, immigrants have come to America over the past centuries not for unrestricted freedom but to use and take advantage of the opportunities offered to work, participate, and improve their lives—to "get ahead," under a system of self-government. This is "ordered liberty" or responsible freedom; what we call in this narrative "noble freedom."

What Freedom Means and Does Not Mean Based on the Values of 1775

It does not mean freedom to:

- Ignore majority rules
- Not work when capable
- Harm others without legal or moral justification
- Be consumed by pleasure or immoral living
- Not participate, i.e., not do your part (rather "do your part with all your heart")

It does mean freedom to:

- Participate in community life and in government rulemaking—including voting, running for office, and speaking or writing your opinions
- Have and enjoy government by the majority (which by itself has certain immutable constraints approved by the people or their forefathers)
- Take advantage of opportunities (pursue happiness) according to the majority-made rules of the game
- Make commitments that are morally and lawfully right
- Worship and practice religion that does not physically harm or physically threaten others

- Own property, work, and do business, as governed by our Common Law and majority-made laws that of course are not unconstitutional.

It certainly means freedom from:

- Arbitrary or unlawful government action
- Taxation without consent
- Rule by the minority
- Overreaching centralized authority (even if elected)
- Restrictions on peaceful religious practices and beliefs
- Unconstitutional laws

This defines noble freedom, a privilege that the minutemen and our founders envisioned for America and for which they fought and died.

Chapter Ten

Radiating Faith

And let us with caution indulge the supposition that morality can be observed without religion.

—George Washington

Religion in 1700 New England

In writing this book, a lingering question was always present. Why did the minutemen have these virtues and values? Where did these come from? What was the cause of the incredible strength of will of our founders? The answer to these questions was discovered when examining their faith in the historical context of those times.

In considering this history, it can be stated with confidant assurance that the American Revolution probably would not have started nor would have been successful if the American people did not possess and practice a strong, mutual, radiating faith that believed both in scripture and in freedom of the individual. To understand the relevance of this faith to the Revolution, it is necessary to recognize the deep and widespread influence and meaning, especially in New England, of the Puritan religious heritage.

Today, as you travel through New England and approach the outskirts of any town, and as seen on countless Christmas cards, you will invariably see in a picturesque valley or on the skyline the tall steeple of a white painted church. This common observation sends everyone a distinct message—New England has a strong religious history. These steeples represent old churches, meetinghouses, around which the towns were first organized in the 1600s and 1700s, though the denominations and beliefs occupying these churches have changed over the years. In the 1700s, almost all of these were "Congregational" meetinghouses. Their pastors' and members' inner convictions were influenced, and their culture and everyday life were molded, by their Puritan heritage. Although the original, strict Puritan culture and doctrines of the mid-1600s had moderated in New England by 1775, many of its beliefs and practices continued to impact churches—both their ministers and members—and the culture. The vast majority of communities in New England functioned within the Puritan sphere of influence.

A typical New England church—the "Meetinghouse" in the 1700s

The Puritan Heritage—the Covenant

To be sure, some original and harsh Puritan practices of the 1600s, such as intolerance of any deviation from Puritanism, cannot stand scrutiny today. Yet many of their core principles have stood the test of time or, at the least, should be respected and honored as worthy American traditions. These Puritan principles included belief in scripture (both Old and New Testaments), the God in scripture, the New Testament's gospel of personal salvation from sin through faith in Christ, the need for personal conversion, prayer, regular meetings in church (the meetinghouse) for worship, singing doctrinally pure hymns every Sunday, making majority-approved decisions, following God's will as they believed it based on scripture, and freedom of the individual (subject of course to the doctrines and beliefs of the church).

All of these convictions essentially expressed themselves in the critically important "*Covenant*," which can be summarized as follows: In gratitude for having received God's promise, or covenant, of salvation by grace through faith in Christ and also because of God's continuing faithfulness to His people, a believer made *both* a voluntary individual commitment, a solemn obligation or covenant, to God, *and* a voluntary, *mutual* promise, also a solemn obligation or covenant, *to each other*, to follow God's will regardless of the cost, to the best of their ability, and with God's help.

Said another way, those of Puritan heritage, which as noted included most residents of New England, believed God forgave and saved them by grace through the Gospel and in return expected them to be obedient to His Word (the Bible), *which they obligated themselves to do.*

Their obligation under the Covenant was to God and each other. It was not the cause of their salvation but rather the effect. God's will *included* the Ten Commandments, acknowledging Christ as Savior, loving those in need that could be helped, being prayerful, thankful, kind and forgiving, exercising self-control, and opposing evil and immorality. It *excluded* envy and greed as well as hatred and murder of anyone including enemies.

The Covenant, though voluntary, was both an individual and a community mindset. In short, it was a mutual, committed, and working faith in the God of the scriptures. Probably the main scripture basis for the Covenant was Matthew 18:20 where Jesus told his disciples, "For where two or three are gathered together in my name, there I am in the midst of them." The Covenant principle extended into all areas of life—as people, from their youth, voluntarily entered into covenants to perform a certain duty or follow majority-approved rules in whatever organization or club they joined or task they performed. It seems to have been as commonplace in New England culture in 1775 as is watching TV or using the internet is in America today. It was the greatest and most far-reaching "app" of those past generations.

Additionally, arising in large measure from their dedication and commitment under the Covenant and probably contributing to the success of the Revolution, the Puritans had a strong "Puritan Work Ethic." This biblical principle was their part of the more well known "Protestant Work Ethic"—in itself a strong historical force significantly affecting American history and society to this day.

Teachings similar to the Covenant—a Christian's disciplined freedom, obligation to obey the scriptures, and opposition to evil—though not as culture-dominating as in New England, were also a strong influence in the middle and southern colonies among the Dutch Reformed, Presbyterians, Lutherans, Baptists, and Methodists. In Virginia, even though the Anglican Church (the Church of England) was the official religion, "dissenting" Protestant congregations at the time of the Revolution were widespread and influential, even outnumbering Anglican churches.

We will now look at some of these Puritan values and discuss how they impacted the Battle of Lexington and the American Revolution—and how they should and could impact people's lives today.

Belief in God

America possesses a chosen country…enlightened by a benign religion, professed, indeed, and practiced in various forms, yet all of them inculcating honesty, truth, temperance, gratitude and the love of man; acknowledging and adoring an overruling Providence, which by all its dispensations proves that it delights in the happiness of man and his greater happiness hereafter.

—Thomas Jefferson

Puritans did not believe in a generic, unknown god but rather the God as described in scripture. More precisely, they believed and feared the God revealed in the Bible. A product of the Reformation, Puritans were essentially Calvinistic in their thinking—and so were determined to understand and follow God's "predetermined will" for their personal lives. Fearing God and honoring the Bible, they did not trust man-made rules inconsistent with scripture and viewed with suspicion all dictates by hereditary rulers or entrenched parliaments.

He shall purify.

—Handel's Messiah, 1742

Unlike the Pilgrims who preceded them in the journey to America for religious freedom, Puritans did not teach a total rejection of the Anglican Church, the established Church of England. Instead, as their name suggests, Puritans sought to reform or purify the Anglican Church of all residual vestiges of the Roman church, such as the use of icons, crucifixes, images, ritualistic liturgy, formalistic prayers, and especially concentrated control. The Pilgrims were "Separatists" while the Puritans were "Dissenters." The Puritans' zeal to "purify" the church also led to their resistance to any restrictions, imposed by the Anglican

Church, on freedom to think and act as the Puritans saw fit according to the scriptures.

So they believed in "freedom" from the centralized practices of the Anglican Church—and over time this conviction of individual Christian freedom transformed into a belief in freedom from all authoritarian, nonrepresented rule. Because of their Puritan heritage and self-governing tradition, the strong desire for freedom from arbitrary secular government was a natural and almost inevitable progression in thought. The courageous flight of both the Pilgrims and later the Puritans to America in the early 1600's is a striking example of this strong inner conviction in personal freedom, both religious and political. The self-defense resistance at the Battle of Lexington is also an example of their view of liberty as a sacred right.

Reason and experience both forbid us to expect that national morality can prevail in exclusion of religious principle

—George Washington

But their belief in political and religious liberty, which over many years became almost an instinct, did not mean, as one without knowledge of their heritage might expect, that everyone could do simply as they please. Puritans did not by any means encourage unlimited, violent, undisciplined, or hedonistic personal freedom. Very much the opposite! Their freedom was to be guided and restrained by the Covenant and by self-government. They believed this so strongly that laws were enacted (by majority vote of course) to compel church attendance (where the scripture and the Covenant were preached) and observance of the Sabbath (Sunday).

Congregational Churches were organized under the principle that the leadership of each church was elected in meetings of the members and important decisions were to be made by majority vote of the members in the meetinghouse. Their towns were also basically governed by town meetings (held in the meetinghouse) where, again, majority vote ruled and all "freemen" were allowed to vote. Following congregational practice, militia companies themselves were also mini-democracies—which is why Captain Parker summoned his men and boys to the Common in order to "consult what to do."

Faith in Scripture

To learn God's will for their lives, that is, to try to live a godly life, Puritans automatically turned, based on their Reformation theology, to the books and teachings of scripture. They believed scripture was the very Word of God with its own divine power, wisdom, and inspiration. (Interesting evidence of their faith in scripture can be found in the first names of the Lexington minutemen—most of these were biblical.) The overriding importance of scripture led directly and logically to the requirement that all children, boys as well as girls, learn to read so that, as adults, they could read and understand the Bible for themselves. This was to give them the knowledge and tools to recognize and avoid false, "satanic," or nonbiblical teachings that might be taught by a pastor or bishop or anyone else. An important and positive side-effect of requiring everyone to read was widespread literacy in America for both men and women. This in turn naturally led to advancements in all fields of human endeavor.

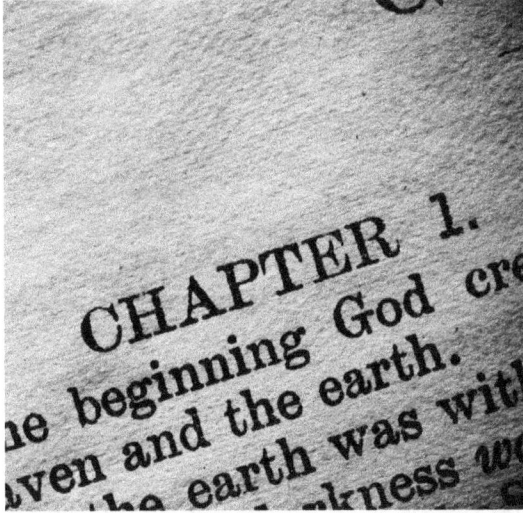

The Puritans studied the Bible carefully and tried to follow its teachings.

Thus the Bible was basic to everything they believed and practiced. And, as we have seen, religious freedom and political freedom gradually and permanently merged into one and the same idea. This is shown by the preaching of the Congregational ministers before the start of the Revolutionary War. They likened the colonists in America, oppressed as they were by the King of England and the English Parliament, to the biblical people of Israel who were slaves in Egypt. The English King was likened to the biblical Pharaoh. Consequently, it was reasoned that the colonists, even though "sinners" like the Israelites, were perfectly justified in defending themselves against British attacks on their property, families, and freedom.

Sam Adams, a dedicated Puritan all of his life, believed and argued with unshakable conviction that political freedom was a proper, even necessary, religious goal for Christians. His reasoning was that subjection to tyranny and surrender to attacks on freedom would directly lead, in addition to political enslavement, to religious persecution of non-Anglican Protestants and the constraint, and eventual destruction, of freedom to worship as they believed. In short, he equated political and religious liberty. He was not alone, as it appears the Puritans of New England were convinced that political despotism would inevitably result in the destruction of religious freedom.

Belief in Prayer

And the longer I live the more convincing proofs I see of this truth, that God governs in the affairs of men. And if a sparrow cannot fall to the ground without his notice, is it possible that an empire can rise without his aid?

—Ben Franklin (raised a Puritan in Boston before moving to Philadelphia at age seventeen), said this in support of his recommendation in 1787 (at age eighty-two) that the Constitutional Convention begin each session with a clergyman's prayer.

Let us beseech God to endue us with all the Christian spirit of piety.

—Sam Adams (paraphrased)

An inevitable result of belief in God and in scriptures was the Puritans' faith in prayer. This was true not only because scripture prolifically teaches the necessity of prayer but also because Puritans recognized that, as part of the Covenant, they needed and would receive through prayer the help of God, who in scripture is described as "almighty" in all of life and death. Not much more needs to be said about their belief in prayer other than this: The Puritans were a praying people.

This means, of course, that prayer, not ritualistic but rather spontaneous "from the heart" prayer, was a daily observance in every home and a weekly practice every Sunday in the meetinghouse. And it was part of the life of the minutemen. There is historical evidence that Congregational ministers led minutemen and militia companies in prayer before they engaged in training exercises—and it seems certain that this practice occurred, if time allowed, before they went on a mission.

Prayer Before Battle

As earlier described, Reverend Jonas Clarke, the minister of the Lexington Congregational Church, probably visited the militia on the Lexington Common sometime between 2:00 am and 3:00 a.m. on April 19, 1775, before the battle. It is quite likely, then, that after briefly speaking to Captain Parker, Reverend Clarke led the militia in a short prayer fitting for that historic occasion and reflecting the simple faith of their Puritan ancestors.

We have no record of the prayer that might have been given by Reverend Clarke on that April 19. And it must be kept in mind he was a great and dedicated patriot leader of his time and a highly regarded, longtime minister of his church (he served the Lexington congregation for fifty years). Because of this, if he did lead the militia company in prayer, it is not to be understood that the quality and full power of words he may have used can be replicated here. Yet, based on his sermon preached a year later, he might have expressed his prayer that morning in words such as the following:

> "O Sovereign God, Governor of nations, we bow with reverence and humility before Thy throne of mercy and goodness. O Lord we know Thou loveth righteousness and hateth iniquity. We acknowledge O Lord we have sinned and deserve Thy holy discipline as did Thy people of old. Yet we also know Thou careth for Thy Church and Thy covenant people. We beseech Thee O Lord, after we suffer the affliction and correction of Thy discipline, that Thou would visit upon us Thy goodness and Thy merciful reformation. In this early morning hour and in these days of perplexity and darkness, we humbly ask Thou wouldst dwell in the midst of these men who boldly stand in unity to oppose those who would oppress

Thy people with bloodthirsty violence. Strengthen these men and their Captain in the coming hours with Thy blessings of faithfulness, covenant obedience, and fortitude. Let them understand, O Lord, they stand here not only for us who are with them now but for this whole land and nation. Grant this, O God, in thy infinite mercy, for the sake of Jesus Christ. Amen"

Going to the Meetinghouse

It is true that church attendance was required by law in most of New England during the pre-revolutionary period. But apparently little attention was given to strict legal enforcement of this law in the late 1700s—and people probably attended church primarily because of habit, Puritan custom, and of course the Covenant. Families as a whole went to church regardless of the weather or distance to be traveled. As required by the Fourth Commandment (and by law), people also did not work on Sundays. Serving the sick and doing only the basic, necessary chores was not considered work.

The content of church services in the meetinghouse was not unlike those in present-day Christian churches—with Scripture reading, a sermon, singing hymns, reading of the Ten Commandments, prayer, learning the "Catechism," baptism, and holy communion.

Hymns of the Lexington Minutemen

Surprisingly, many of the hymns sung in that time are still very much in use today—particularly those of Isaac Watts, who, along with Charles Wesley, is considered one of the greatest hymn writers who ever lived. Watts, born in 1674 and writing his hymns in the early 1700s in England, was himself a "Dissenter" from the Anglican Church—meaning that he was cut from the same cloth as Puritans and followed their beliefs. Many of his hymns, which totaled well over 500, were sung by American churches of that day (and of today), including of course the Lexington Congregational Church.

Some of Isaac Watts' familiar hymns, certainly known and sung by the Lexington congregation, include:

Joy to the World

When I Survey the Wondrous Cross

Come Holy Spirit, Heavenly Dove

Am I a Soldier of the Cross

Jesus Shall Reign Where'er the Sun

I Sing the Mighty Power of God

The hymns of Isaac Watts were scripture-based—undoubtedly to the liking of Bible-believing Puritans in New England. His greatest and best-known hymn, also familiar and sung during that time, "*O God Our Help in Ages Past,*" is based on Psalm 90. As is true with this hymn, he wrote many hymns that followed the Old Testament Psalms, but worded them to reflect beliefs and teachings from the New Testament. For example, "*Joy to the World,*" today a favorite Christmas carol, is based on Psalm 98.

Statue of Isaac Watts. In the 1700s, his scripture-based hymns were sung by Puritans including the minutemen.

O God Our Help in Ages Past

If you set aside this book for a moment and gaze out a window toward whatever nature you can see (a tree, a field, a garden, a flower, a child at play) and then close your eyes and imagine a New England meetinghouse full of worshippers, you may be able to hear, deep in your heart, the Lexington congregation, gathered together, powerfully and distinctly singing "*O God Our Help in Ages Past*" on Sunday morning, April 14, 1775. In this hymn, you may notice the Covenant references to "our" and "we" and to God as the almighty protector and guide of believers.

O God our help in ages past,
Our hope for years to come.
Our shelter from the stormy blast,
And our eternal home.

Under the shadow of Thy throne
Still may we dwell secure.
Sufficient is Thine arm alone,
And our defense is sure.

Before the hills in order stood
Or earth received her frame.
From everlasting Thou art God,
To endless years the same.

A thousand ages in Thy sight
Are like an evening gone.
Short as the watch that ends the night,
Before the rising sun.

Time, like an ever-rolling stream
Bears all its sons away.
They fly forgotten as a dream,
Dies at the opening day.

O God our help in ages past,
Our hope for years to come.
Be Thou our guide while life shall last,
And our eternal home.

Going to Church (the Meetinghouse) and the Revolution

What importance does Puritan church attendance have for the American Revolution and the events of April 19, 1775? First, the people attending services at the meetinghouse, which was nearly everyone in town, learned from their ministers and from scripture the importance of freedom— from both religious and political "slavery." Freedom to worship according to their own scripture-based rules, to make their own laws and elect their own leaders was both inherent and explicit in the teaching of the churches and considered a basic spiritual right more valuable than life itself. So when the British rashly attempted to stifle colonial personal liberty and to destroy self-governing rights with military force, they stirred up a huge spiritual hornet's nest— and all residents of Lexington and of most other towns were willing to oppose, at the cost of their lives, the invasion or "oppression" of the British Regulars.

Secondly, going to the meetinghouse not only was part of community life, this custom supported and probably was the primary cause of a productive community culture. Virtually all people were part of something. Their church and the Covenant had deep meaning and importance for them— derived from the scripture readings, sermons, and hymns which they were exposed to and participated in every Sunday. This spiritual strength, almost steel-like in its power and growing out of the Covenant, in turn seemed to cause people to support each other and go along with community decisions—such as joining the militia and sternly opposing any Loyalist sentiments.

Thirdly, people attending church learned from their minister that they, as Covenant believers, were people of

God, much like the biblical Israelites. It followed that the defense of their homes, families, church, and way of life was, although regretful, absolutely necessary when forcibly attacked by "oppressors." And God would help them!

Radiating Faith on April 19, 1775— Lessons For Today

I wish we were a more religious people

—Sam Adams after the Revolution

It would not be accurate to say the colonists of New England having a Puritan heritage were saintly or near-perfect in morality and in social or political relations. Conflicts, mistakes, sins, failures, and problems abounded. But they fully understood, and were continually made conscious of, the utmost importance in striving for obedience to scripture teachings of morality and self-discipline as required by the Covenant, as expounded by their ministers, and as they understood it for themselves.

Puritans, as people of the Covenant, were exhorted and expected to follow the scriptures, serve God, and help their fellow man. They did not advocate hatred, aggression, or murder. Although the early Puritans of the 1600s had a deserved reputation for rigidity in attitude and intolerance of non-Puritan beliefs, this reputation in 1775 was no longer accurate. For example, if a citizen said he could not adhere to the full Covenant, he was afforded the right to a "Halfway Covenant"—and then did not have the same obligations as a full church member. Nonetheless, all were urged to follow *strong moral principles* based on their understanding of Old Testament laws and New Testament teachings. It is fair to say most tried the best they could to live by their principles, even if falling short on many occasions.

The Wellspring of Minutemen Virtues and Values

It can be concluded, then, based on the historical accounts of that early period of the Revolutionary War, that Puritan-based faith, the Puritan Covenant, was the wellspring, the source, the very cornerstone, of the other minutemen virtues and values—admirable courage, virtuous reliability, purposeful moral unity, the desire for secure peace, and noble freedom—that in turn led to their willingness to face the Regulars.

Their courage undoubtedly came from the conviction that God's almighty power would aid them and be with them as they defended their God-given liberty. Their reliability was surely the fruit of the Puritan Work Ethic—arising equally from their personal unwavering obligation to the Covenant and from learning, in the meetinghouse, the importance of conscientious obedience to God and his commandments. Their unity sprang from their faithful habit of going to church meetings in the meetinghouse and being part of one Covenant group, a congregation, with singleness of purpose, worthy values, and shared mutual obligations. And without question their desire for secure peace was learned from scripture, where it is taught that God desires peace on earth and peace with God in one's heart. Similarly, the value of noble freedom undoubtedly arose from their work ethic, from accepting majority vote for regulating their lives, from the Covenant, and from their belief in the Ten Commandments and in an omnipresent God who saw and knew what they did. It is worthy of note that the men illustrating the individual examples of personal virtues and values cited in this book—the Lexington minutemen, Captain John Parker, Paul Revere, Sam Adams, and John Hancock—all were Puritans in their heritage and in their way of life.

Why Not Today?

What would happen if everyone, as the minutemen, believed in and feared the God of the sacred scriptures and were motivated by an inner belief in the grace of God and a solemn obligation, a "covenant? Their behavior would be sculptured to:

- Honor their voluntary commitments to God, each other, and society;

- Read, study, and take to heart the scriptures to the best of their ability;

- Meet in church, where scripture-founded hymns of praise and inspiration are sung and where the scripture and gospel with its message of love and grace are clearly and carefully explained; and

- Pray in their homes and in churches with the trust and confidence that they were petitioning an "Almighty God."

This is what was happening in 1775 in Lexington, Massachusetts! For those in America today who do not accept scripture as divinely inspired, perhaps they might acknowledge the validity and power of core moral values as evidenced by, or comparable to, Biblical truths. Scripture, after all, can be held up as presenting stable principles tested by centuries of time -- principles accepted by many of the greatest people who have ever lived (Abraham Lincoln, George Washington, Martin Luther King, Thomas Jefferson, Winston Churchill, Martin Luther, John Calvin, Saint Augustine, to name a few) Who can make corrections to scripture, whose intelligence or education is of more value, or whose insight or wisdom is more penetrating and enduring?

When the minutemen did their best to follow a mutual covenant centered around basic tenets of morality, the outcome for America was admirable courage, purposeful moral unity, virtuous reliability, the desire for true peace, and noble freedom! For this freedom to endure, these virtues and values need to be renewed and lived again.

The Strength of Pluralities

But is this goal really achievable with the present-day wide plurality of beliefs (and non-belief)? Is a moral covenant comparable to the one that motivated the Lexington minutemen, totally unrealistic today and even insulting to people with different values? We can confidently say the answer is no! Other peaceful religions and beliefs have many virtues that are worthy and moral in their purposes. These religions can strengthen their own commitment, their personal and mutual obligation, to pursue admirable courage, purposeful moral unity, virtuous reliability, a desire for secure peace, and noble freedom.

Moreover, the plurality of ethnic groups and religions in America has been and can be a source of great strength rather than a cause of weakness. No culture, religion, or worldview as *actually lived* by human beings is perfect—and the strengths, the virtues, of one, as practiced, can complement, help, and even point out the shortcomings of another as it is practiced. Who of us having a good conscience cannot recognize a worthy virtue when we see it practiced? And a valuable lesson can then be learned and the fibre of our country will be strengthened!

And certainly those of us who ascribe to the Christian faith can rededicate and commit ourselves (make a covenant!) as Christians to meet our obligations to each other, to honor the simple faith of belief in the God of the scriptures and the gospel, and to meet together regularly in worship and prayer to learn God's will for life—from the teachings of scripture and from the beliefs of the historic Christian church as taught by ministers and leaders who themselves believe in scripture and in the historic beliefs of Christianity.

A New Sunrise for America

The smiles of heaven can never be expected on a nation that disregards the eternal rules of order and right which heaven itself has ordained.

—George Washington

I would submit, therefore, that our present-day world would be a far better place if the virtues and values of the Lexington minutemen and our patriot founding fathers were voluntarily renewed in American culture. A new golden age of America would dawn, a hopeful and even more brilliant sunrise than April 19, 1775.

Virtuous reliability would undoubtedly cause a decrease in the crime rate. This same virtue would also strike a blow against the abuse of drugs and alcohol and other destructive habits.

Purposeful moral unity would significantly lessen political and family dissension, and unified citizens would accomplish surprising good for our nation and our communities Businessmen and employees (and husbands and wives and families) would be more compatible and less self-centered because of the desire for a secure peace.

Exercising noble freedom and virtuous reliability would cause a decline in school drop out rates and unemployment. These two virtues would in addition reverse trends of unjust discrimination while at the same time making employees and students more responsible and punctual. Using noble freedom would increase responsible and productive participation in the economy, government and civic groups.

Most importantly, in following the virtue of admirable courage, we would see and achieve, for the blessing of mankind, a decline in violence, intentional injury, and physical abuse along with their lasting consequences.

Returning then, with divine aid, to its moral foundation, America and its freedom will be worthy of God's eternal grace and protection.

Oh make Thou us, through centuries long,
In peace secure, in justice strong;
Around our gift of freedom draw
The safeguards of Thy righteous law;
And, cast in some diviner mould,
Let the new cycle shame the old!

—John Greenleaf Whittier, "Centennial Hymn"

Sure I must fight, if I would reign;
Increase my courage, Lord:
I'll bear the toil, endure the pain,
Supported by Thy Word.

—Isaac Watts, "Am I a Soldier of the Cross"

Were the whole real of nature mine,
That were a present far too small;
Love so amazing, so divine,
Demands my soul, my life, my all.

—Isaac Watts, "When I Survey the Wondrous Cross"

O God our help in ages past,
Our hope for years to come.
Be Thou our guide while life shall last,
And our eternal home.

Bibliography and Sources

Books

Blum, John M., Bruce Catton, Edmund S. Morgan, Arthur M. Schlesinger, Jr., Kenneth M. Stampp, C. Vann Woodward. *The National Experience, A History of the United States,* Second Edition. New York: Harcourt, Brace and World, Inc., 1968.

Campbell, Norine Dickson. *Patrick Henry: Patriot and Statesman.* Old Greenwich, CT: The Devin-Adair Company, 1969.

Brands, H. W. *The First American: The Life and Times of Benjamin Franklin.* New York: Anchor Books, 2000.

Clark, Pastor Jonas. *The Battle of Lexington: A Sermon & Eyewitness Narrative (Originally Titled: The Fate of Blood-Thirsty Oppressors and God's Tender Care of His Distressed People).* Ventura, CA: Nordskog Publishing, 2007.

Davis, Kenneth C. *America's Hidden History.* New York: Harper Collins, 2009.

Earle, Alice Morse. *Home Life in Colonial Days.* Mineola, NY: Dover Publications, 2006 (originally published 1998).

Fischer, David Hackett. *Paul Revere's Ride.* New York: Oxford University Press, 1994.

Fleming, Thomas. *Liberty! The American Revolution.* New York: The Penguin Group, 1997.

Gross, Robert A. The *Minutemen and Their World.* New York: Hill and Wang, 1981.

Hawke, David Freeman. *Everyday Life in Early America.* New York: Harper & Row, 1998.

Kaminsky, John P. *The Quotable Jefferson.* Princeton, NJ: Princeton University Press, 2006.

Langguth, A. J. *Patriots: The Men Who Started the American Revolution.* New York: Simon & Schuster, 1988.

McCullough, David. *John Adams.* New York: Simon & Schuster, 2001.

Nevins, Allan and Henry Steele Commager. *A Short History of the United States.* New York: The Modern Library (Random House), 1956.

Newsweek Book, Editors. *The Founding Fathers: Thomas Jefferson, A Biography in His Own Words*, Volume I. New York: Newsweek Books, 1974.

Paine, Thomas. *Common Sense and The Crisis.* New York: Anchor Books, 1973.

Raphael, Ray. *The First American Revolution Before Lexington and Concord.* New York: The New Press, 2002.

Stoll, Ira. *Samuel Adams: A Life.* New York: Free Press, 2008.

Taylor, Dale. *The Writer's Guide to Everyday Life in Colonial America.* Cincinnati: Writer's Digest Books, 1997.

Tourtellot, Arthur B. *Lexington and Concord. The Beginning of the War of the American Revolution.* New York: W.W. Norton & Company, Inc., 1959.

Waldman, Michael. *My Fellow Americans: The Most Important Speeches of America's Presidents, from George Washington to George W. Bush.* Naperville, IL: Sourcebooks, Inc., 2003.

Whittier, John Greenleaf. *The Complete Poetical Works.* New York: Grosset & Dunlap, 1892.

Other Sources

Library of Congress. Journals of the Continental Congress, May 1775.

Library of Congress. Affidavits of Witnesses to the Commencement of Hostilities Presented and Read before the Continental Congress, May 1775.

Paul Revere's Deposition for the Massachusetts Provincial Congress, 1775.

Paul Revere's Letter to Jeremy Belknap, 1798.

"Official Account" of the March of the British Troops and List of the Provincials Who Were Killed and Wounded by the British Troops, April 25, 1775.

www.ingramcontent.com/pod-product-compliance
Lightning Source LLC
Chambersburg PA
CBHW020514100426
42813CB00030B/3247/J